WOMEN AND LAW

WOMEN AND LAW

Rameshwari Pandya

MADHAV BOOKS
GURGAON (HARYANA)

First Published - 2009

ISBN: 978-81-907891-3-4

Published by

MADHAV BOOKS
F-2562, Palam Vihar
Gurgaon-122 017 (Haryana)
Phone : 0124-2365193, 9810373248

Contents

Acknowledgments

It was a great privilege to work under the able guidance of Dr. Arvinda Chandra, Professor, Department of Education and Extension. I would like to convey my deepest gratitude for all her systematic guidance, constant advice and wise suggestions and support in conducting this research.

The valuable suggestions and advice provided by Dr. Anupama Shah, Head, Department of Education and Extension, is sincerely acknowledged. I am also grateful to all the experts from the Faculty of Home Science, Centre of Advance Study in Education, Department of Psychology, Baroda, and Indian Space Research Organisation, Ahmedabad, for all their help and support. My thanks also to all the experts for their valuable suggestions at the time of validation of tool.

With warm gratitude I acknowledge the co-operation extended by the teachers teaching the first year students in the Faculty of Home Science, M.S. University of Baroda, who helped to make it possible for me to carry out the experiments during some of their classes.

I also acknowledge the co-operation extended to me by the first year students without which it would not have been possible to carry out the experiment of the present study.

I express my special thanks to Dr. N.S. Pathak, Dean, Faculty of Education and Psychology, Baroda, for his help and suggestions in statistical analyses.

My sincere thanks to Ms. Geeta Parikn and Mr. Atul Mehta, lawyers, in the District Court of Baroda, for their valuable help and guidance.

I extend my thanks to Mr. Ilesh Vyas and Mr. Satyan for shooting, editing and in preparations of the video films.

I am thankful to Mr. Kalpesh Pandya, Asst. Technician of the Department of Home Science Education and Extension, in arranging the video film shows.

Mr. K.K. Bansal deserves credit for the help he provided in computerising the data.

I am grateful to my husband Dr. Mahesh Pandya for his everwilling help and support in various phases of the research.

I extend my profound thanks to him and my dear sons Siddhartha and Shrikanth whose love and sacrifice was the source of encouragement for the completion of my Ph.D. programme.

I am in loss of words to express my deepest gratitude and appreciation to my mother and father. Their encouragement, unending motivation and help acted as a constant source of inspiration to me and my work. I take this opportunity to convey heartful thanks to them for their never failing love.

RAMESHWARI PANDYA

Chapter 1

Introduction

Women have been idolised in India and yet they have also been exploited and denied social justice. This is seen in the increasing incidents of violence on women. In recent years, violence against women has become increasingly visible and an important social issue. Police officials, lawyers, social workers, policy makers and educationists are of the opinion that only a small number of incidents, especially those involving severe injury or death, get newspaper and media coverage.

There are social, cultural and economic factors which combine to compel Indian women to play the role of silent victims of violence. All Indian laws get their sanction from the Indian Constitution which guarantees justice, liberty and equality to all citizens of India. The preamble speaks of equality of status and of opportunity for all citizens. Article 14 of the Indian Constitution states that "The State shall not deny to any person equality before the law or the equal protection of the laws within the territory of India".

The Constitution, however, is a document at a high level of abstraction. It is the guiding document of the State. The Indian Constitution is remarkable for its clear-cut emphasis towards justice and equality for all. Women in particular, are recognised by the Constitution as weak and vulnerable, therefore are to be given special protection.

The Constitution has guaranteed equality to women not only before the law, but also in education, in providing equal opportunities and in public appointments. Women have been made an integral part of the Constitution so that the goals of justice-social, economic and political equality of opportunity for all, can be achieved. Furthermore the Constitution makes special provisions for women to help them improve their social status in society.

In the Planning process, under the trickle down theory, it was expected that women will equally benefit along with men. This has been belied by actual developments. The Sixth Plan Document recognises that "in spite of the Constitutional legal equality given to women, they have lagged behind in almost all sectors". In the past decade, there have been various forces and pressures which have pushed women into a low and inferior place. These forces have been more dominant than those which should have tried to bring up women towards growth and development.

Whether legislation exists or does not exist, the benefits are virtually zero. For many women the laws are non-existent or, if existing, insignificant, ill-conceived, delayed or simply not implemented for the women. Though several ameliorative legal provisions have been passed for the welfare of women, they continue to suffer. There is a big gap in the enactment of legal provisions and the benefits reaching the women. Lack of awareness of the rights and lack of knowledge of law is the reason why women continue to be mute victims of an unjust and irrational society.

In short, despite the amendments in laws over a period of time, the advantages of laws have not been used to its fullest which can be attributed to the lack of proper under-standing of the law by the women. That is the reason crime rate is on an increase.

It is indeed sad that whatever changes and amendments, have been made, for the improvement of the legal status of women, have not reached them. The benefits have not reached due to lack of awareness of the beneficiaries as stated in several studies.

To a lay person a law is very strange-something distant and incomprehensible. If the law says so, it is irrevocably right and just, even though apparently it may not be so. In the case of women, basically there is injustice built into the system, or justice which has not been brought out forcefully, nor often enough. It is not enough to pass a law. There should be continuous education of the people, for the real purpose behind the various laws so that they themselves can become the epitomes of law and justice.

The laws are seen to remain a dead letter until there is pressure for its implementation. There are many examples all over the country where progressive laws exist but have had no impact because they remain unimplemented.

The findings of the various studies and the observations made by the Joshi Committee on software, confirm the invisibility of women. T.V., the medium which is supposed to educate and inform, has very little information about the actual condition of women. (Shramskati 1987, p. 189).

Women are provided beauty tips, but no advice is given to women who are unhappy in their marital home, on how they should take help from the law. Advice is given on how to be a good wife and a good mother by making adjustments within the family situation.

Doordarshan repeatedly portrays women as house bound engaged in homemaking entirely dependent for their existence and fulfillment on their husbands and children. The struggle that women are facing for economic and political autonomy, legal rights and identity is almost completely ignored.

> "Laws relating to women are rarely covered in the media and issues related to women are let out. It rarely receive the necessary exposure, so that at least through word-of-mouth, information may trickle down from one literate, informed women to another. Women's plight, hardly seem newsworthy matters. Even when media attention is given they are usually sensationalised with headlines such as 'Minor raped in K.E.M. Hospital." (Shramskati 1987, p. 179)

There is an attempt in print media to maintain the status quo, and counteract good articles on women with negative ideas and images. For example, an article on harassment of women may be subsequently trivialised by a light-hearted account on 'eve teasing' highlighted by a cartoon.

However, lately radio, television and other mass communication media have exposed the women to information and knowledge about legal provisions. However, such exposures have not yet resulted in creating consciousness to the desired extent among women, nor have they succeeded in loosening the hold of tradition-oriented thinking of the masses.

Over the last two decades, due to the constant campaigns of women's groups and the overall impact of the women's decade, which was declared by U.N.O., there has been a steady increase of serious coverage on women's issues. This is also because women themselves are becoming articulate bold and expressive. Issues such as violence, dowry and sexual harassment, which were at one time dismissed as the problems of an individual woman, are being seen within socio-political structural context. The result is that, there is an awareness in the print media with women wishing to discuss problems such as gender insubordination, social and sexual exploitation, legal disabilities and wage discrimination. Committed individuals and groups are leaving no stone unturned to get the message to the concerned persons.

> "By and large, women have been ignored or treated as sex objects. Attempts have been made by freelance journalists, activists, academicians and concerned staff to counteract these features."
>
> (Shramskati 1987, p. 202)

Some research organisations also produce journals and newsletters wherein information about women in the organized sector is disseminated and for the first time, attention has been drawn to the oppressive conditions of women in India.

> "The Commission strongly recommends a special drive for imparting legal literacy to women so as to enable them to be aware of the existing legislations and the methodologies through which they can take benefit under the legislation."
>
> (Shramskati 1987, p. 293)

The struggle for legal equality has been one of the major concerns of women movement all over the world. Whether in the internal situation of her position in the parental or matrilineal home or in the external situation of acquiring education, skills, profession, employment, all these involve law. Even best of the intentions to generate an atmosphere of equality can not easily overcome the thousands of years of social distance perpetrated by caste, class, community and gender differences.

Women themselves need to develop a self identity so that they can lead a life of security and dignity. This can be achieved by making them aware of their legal rights and potentials. A number of social enactments have been put on the status books for removing various constraints which hinder women's progress. Inspite of these measures, women have been lagged behind by men in different spheres.

There has been, in general, a lack of awareness among the people about various legislations and programmes being implemented for the benefit of women. United Nations sponsored "World Conference on Women" held in Nairobi, Kenya, July, 1985, declared :

> Legal education is essential, for the full realisation of equality among women and men. Obstacles to equality should be eliminated by introducing general knowledge of the law in curriculum.

IMPORTANCE OF VIDEO

In the 20th century, communication technology has made tremendous strides. It is now theoretically possible to reach the remotest corners of the earth. The importance of video as an alternate medium has been greatly realised in recent years. Many grass root organisations, academic institutions and invididuals are using video cassettes to provide information to make the viewers aware of the rights and opportunities. SEWA video, health groups like CHETNA, CENDIT (Centre for the Development of Instructional Technology), ASTHA, St. Xaviers communications group, are a few illustrative names which are involved in producing theme-based purposeful video programmes which are shown to the women groups to create awareness.

The communication technology for development ranges from the simple to the most complicated forms. One such form which has the potential to reach at individual and family levels and act with full force, appeal and flexibility is video.

Gupta (1983) explained that one of the major features of informational society is video technology. It has become more popular than other media due to easy mobility and increased accessibility. Video cassette recorder and player, being a hand tool is simple to operate. It has the potential to educate, inform and entertain each individual member in the family. Therefore, it has become very visible and all pervasive in the lives of a large number of people.

According to Bhagat (1988) there are mechanical advantages of modern communication technology, to transmit the latest information at low cost to a very large number of people of all ages, even in remote areas where general communication and educational facilities do not exist.

In the last few decades of the current century, technology has influenced human life greatly. For the fast and overall development of India, there is an immediate need to identify the use of the latest technologies on one hand and identification of the role of software on the other.

Tiwari (1985) writes

> The challenge, therefore, is really for the artists, poets, writers, thinkers, humanists, sociologists, art historians and culture critics, who must join

> together and provide a vision and insight for ushering in a new life in our country by providing relevant software for the latest communication technology. (Tiwari 1985, p. 2)

Seymour (1973) adopted video cassette as a standard output format for audio-visuals for Research and Development Centre for Teacher Education and Major Educational Research Centres of University of Texas, Austin, considering the following advantages.

- *User Convenience*: Video cassettes cannot be erased accidentally. The video cassettes may be stopped, rewound, replayed or even removed at any point in the playing cycle.
- *Input Versatility*: With input formats duplicate VC, cost substantially less than duplicates of the product made in the original medium.
- *Room light viewing*: High quality T.V. picture produced by a cassette player can be watched by the teacher and students in full room light in day-time. They may take legible notes.
- *Viewing habits*: Student are accustomed to watching T.V., it is their familiar habit.
- *Reuse of material*: Video cassettes can be reused over and over again with a view to futuristic perspectives.

Considering these advantages investigator selected video cassettes as the teaching aids.

According to P.O.A. (1986), education requires media support which is related to the curriculum. Video technology offers considerable potential for improvement of the quality of education.

Video has the potential to educate. The education can only be effective, if the medium is utilized more imaginatively. Advantage of video are many as it has the facility of reviewing cassettes makes it cheap and cost effective if video film and programme needs to be viewed again and again. The rewinding and forwarding mechanisms in video are assets, that add to critical viewing for full understanding and enjoyment of the programme.

As far as ease in operation is concerned, video has easy handling and functional mechanism which any one will feel confident to do. Furthermore, its portability is another advantageous factor.

Video is an ideal medium to convey information to both illiterate and literate urban and rural viewers.

Video can cater to the needs of a variety of groups, and hence, its wise use can uplift the standard of the neglected groups. One such neglected group in India is that of women, although basically in the family or home the key figure is the woman.

In the past, society has recognized their unique contribution as wives and mothers. Women's role and status in the society should not be neglected, as they are significant pointers to the level of culture of the society and they could be the most powerful channel for development. Therefore, it is time to help them understand their role as citizens. They are amongst the most underdeveloped, illiterate and exploited segments of Indian society though they constitute half of India's population. Moreover, they also face the problem of illiteracy and ignorance.

Due to higher education, the outlook of the college educated homemakers would in turn result to increase in alertness towards the rights of the women and children. Furthermore, there would be drastic changes in their attitudes and they may become more alert about the laws and legislation affecting women's rights and privileges and thus emancipation of women, which will help in improving the status of women. Another possibility that is the college educated women will become conscious of themselves and potentials which they have. Hence, they will participate in national development as informed, participating citizens.

JUSTIFICATION FOR THE STUDY

Need For Legal Education In Home Science

The Faculty of Home Science imparts education in five major areas viz. Child Development, Clothing and Textiles, Home Management, Home Science Education and Extension and Food and Nutrition. There are lot of preconceived notions and prejudices regarding Home Science. To many it connotes the preparation of a girl to "run a home in an ideal manner and be a good housewife". However, this is not the only objective, because as a discipline it encompasses a wide range of subjects. Home Science promotes the overall development of an individual. Despite its broad outreach and vast scope it does not deal at all with any aspect of legal education specially pertaining to women. The field of Home Science can be more meaningful and strong and relevant if it incorporates new body of knowledge in its curriculum.

The objectives of Home Science is to develop attitudes and behaviour competency in keeping with the needs of the society. Hence women's education should be planned according to the felt needs of the society.

> Home Science as a discipline of higher education needs to meet the challenges related to improving its academic quality, and secondly, the challenges related to home, family, and individual in the national context. (Chandra 1978, p. 53)

Legal education in Home Science should be considered more seriously than anything else because in recent years crime against women has assumed giant shape. Even facts related to figures on crime serve as an eye opener for Home Scientists whose activities are geared towards betterment of family, community and nation keeping the women as their focus.

Among the need which the individual is facing, the need of acquiring legal protection in times of crisis, is a great one. The role of women has become wider and complex and a satisfying role enactment requires knowledge of law. Home

Science, today is inadequate without inclusion of legal knowledge in its curricula.

The University Grants Commission has also emphatically recommended guidelines for restructuring and reviewing courses so that new ideas, concepts, content and structure can be incorporated. It has suggested that the courses at college should have more application-oriented components.

The National Policy of Education (1986) has also laid special emphasis on the education of women and suggested reviewing and reorganizing the educational activities to ensure that it makes a substantial contribution towards women's equality. Therefore, by introducing a course on women and law, which will make students aware of their legal rights.

The investigator reviewed the literature in the form of reports of Government of India, Seminar and workshop reports, research reports, books, journals and newspaper articles. All these confirm the fact that there are various laws for the benefit of women but because of lack of their awareness, women are victimized.

Today's girls are going to be future women and they may have to face the world where the crime rates are progressively increasing. It, therefore, becomes very important to educate these young girls about their legal rights. This would also help to create awareness, understanding and sensitivity among them. Moreover, the home scientists must use their foresight to prepare women for the time of crises. The general observation and practical experiences of the investigator is that the legal knowledge and awareness among Home Science students is very poor.

The results of the feasibility study conducted by the investigator with a sample of first year Home Science students in March 1990, revealed that students have a positive opinion towards legal education as a course in Home Science. More than 90 per cent respondents agreed that legal education is desirable for Home Science students. Further, the findings showed that, there were only about 40 per cent girls who had correct awareness of the different laws concerning women. The remaining 60 per cent either did not have any awareness or had incorrect awareness.

The feasibility study also supports the need for legal education to be given to Home Science students, because only 10 per cent of the respondents had formal legal education. Majority of the respondents never had a course on legal education in school or outside the school by any other agency. This highlights the need for a formal education system to impart legal education to the girls so that it could be of some help at the time of distress.

Generally one avoids reading about the laws as it is assumed that legal jargon is too difficult to understand and that laws are not pertinent to our lives. Therefore, an introductory course could be planned in simple and understandable language, highlighting the issues relevant to women. Such a course should be introduced elucidating various aspects of laws and legal procedures protecting women's right. It need to be started in Home Science Institutes which has majority of female students. Finally, the investigator feels that the lead for breaking new ground in curriculum matters must come from the group whom it concerns the most. This means the Home Science colleges should address themselves to particular needs of women.

Women's issues have assumed tremendous importance and have been attracting a lot of attention in recent years.

> "There is an imperative need for a concentrated move on the part of both the Central and State governments as well as bodies which seek to organise and activate women to realise their rights and opportunities for development and mobilise them for social change to tap this vast potentiality of human power for gainful utilisation for the good of the family, society and country as a whole by imparting work oriented training with some basic education, bearing in mind that this may have to be taken to the doorsteps of their houses which is now feasible, that with the growth of mass media such as Radio, T.V., Tape Recorder, Video, etc.".
>
> (K. Vasanthi Devi 1985, p. 3)

Need to Develop a Video Package to Teach Parts of the Course on "Women and Law"

Different research studies have proved that the video is an effective medium for teaching. The investigator has selected the video to teach the course "Women and Law" because of the following reasons:

Information

The laws contain lot of information on facts. For example, if a girl is molested by a man and it is proved, then he can be punished. This is an information for a specific situation and similarly other laws have information. Thus informative video film could be used in imparting such legal education.

Figures

Many figures are available on rate of crime against women are available. To highlight some of the facts related to the study of law these figures can be used instead of giving simple lecture. These figures can be more impressive and can be effective if used in the form of video film.

Pictorial Form

The investigator has found that Haksar (1986) has already put forth the idea of using pictorial forms in imparting information on laws. Now if this information is put in the form of video film containing pictures related to law, it may become still more effective.

Conversation

Direct discussion and dialogues form is more effective than traditional lecture form. One teacher alone cannot use all these methods in a class room, whereas this is possible through video film. This is the reason why video film is produced and used by the investigator.

Video is a powerful medium in the hands of teacher to facilitate the teaching. It would enhance the effectiveness of the learning and be as effective as any other projected aids.

It will be an aid to supplement the teaching and not to substitute the teacher.

The mass media are looked upon as an essential element of the production and development process. Video is the newest addition to the already available several powerful media for mass communication. Research studies support the advantages of video.

> Video as compared to other audio visual aids is more effective in enhancing understanding and clarifying concepts. (Chandra, Shah and Thomas, 1987)

Video has several advantages over other conventional methods of communication. Video increases motivation and thereby its use can improve the teaching situation. The investigator is confident that video films can be very useful as an effective medium for introducing the course on "Women and Law" to the first year students of Faculty of Home Science.

It is, therefore, necessary that the course content on "Women and Law" is developed and a video film documenting various laws pertinent to women be used to impart legal education to first year Home Science students.

The need for making a video film is very well expressed in Hopkinson's words (1971), p. 32.

> The viewing screen, in one form or another, is becoming as normal and dependable source of learning as the book. It may be more expensive but is also more often flexible more stimulating and more effective.

Mass Media being no exception with the advent of modern technology available indigenously, all type of media especially the audio visual type have become more popular than any other media due to their easy mobility and increased accessibility. Among the most popular are T.V. and V.C.R. These media are considered very effective tools for mass communication. They provide not only entertainment but also are widely used to disseminate educational information.

They have, therefore, become very visible and all pervasive in the lives of large section of the population. Video has the potential to educate. The education can only be effective, if the medium is utilized more imaginatively. In order to cater to the needs of the women. The content of the Home Science courses to be imparted should be current and pertinent to our lives. Video is the most potent medium for covering such message effectively.

Educational Television can play an important role in the instruction of students where an effective teacher may not be available.

There are a few specialised agencies set up for the development of software for the educational T.V. programmes. They, are:

1. Educational Media Research Centre, (EMRC), Gujarat University, Ahmedabad.
2. E.M.R.C. Poona University, Poona.
3. E.M.R.C. Osmania University, Hyderabad.

There is need for teacher made Video Instructional Package. The teachers are the best judges of what experiences are to be provided and how they should be sequentially organised. It is not enough that the teacher makes such packages but the try out of these programmes are very essential, so that the teacher can provide feedback about the programmes and improve upon the succeeding ones.

Undertaking a study to develop the content of course "Women and Law" in relation to the curriculum of Home Science assumes significance and should be given appropriate priority.

Keeping the above justifications in mind, a study on "Women and Law" is undertaken.

STATEMENT OF THE PROBLEM

Developing a course and a video instructional package on "Women and Law" and measuring the effectiveness of package with the students of Faculty of Home Science, Baroda.

OBJECTIVES OF THE STUDY

Major Objectives

1. To develop an effective introductory course on "Women and Law".
2. To develop video instructional package on "Women and Law".
3. To study the effectiveness of video package to teach "Women and Law" to the first year Home Science students in terms of performance of students on knowledge test.

Specific Objectives

1. To develop an introductory course on "Women and Law" including laws pertaining to women.
2. To study the effectiveness of video package for teaching selected units.
3. To study the effectiveness of video films in terms of students' achievement according to the stream of study at higher secondary school.
4. To study the effectiveness of video films in terms of students' achievement according to the medium of instruction at school.
5. To study the effectiveness of video films in terms of students' achievement according to the place of residence.
6. To study the effectiveness or video films in terms of students' achievement according to their inclination towards social sciences.
7. To study the effectiveness of video films in terms of students' achievement according to their family's legal exposure.
8. To study the effectiveness of video films in terms of students' achievement according to the social work background.
9. To study the effectiveness of video films in terms of students' achievement according to their mother's occupation.

10. To study the effectiveness of video films in terms of students' achievement according to their exposure to TV and video.
11. To study the effectiveness of video films in terms of students' achievement according to the socio-economic status.
12. To study the effectiveness of video films in terms of students' achievement according to the overall modernity.
13. To study the effectiveness of video films in terms of students' achievement according to their personality.
14. To study the effectiveness of video films in terms of students' achievement according to the level of academic achievement.
15. To study the effectiveness of video films in terms of students' achievement according to their English competence.

ASSUMPTIONS

The basic assumptions underlying the present study were as follows.

1. The theoretical content for developing outline and video instructional package on "Women and Law" is available in literature like books, journals, periodicals and magazines.
2. The students will take interest in the video instructional package on "Women and Law".
3. Video is being used as an instructional strategy for formal teaching.
4. The group size of the class is suitable enough to conduct the experiment.
5. The students will be able to respond to structured questionnaire on "Women and Law".
6. The effect of learning can be measured in terms of knowledge after teaching experimental units of the course "Women and Law".

NULL HYPOTHESES

1. There will be no significant difference in knowledge gain in terms of pre-post scores of the students according to the stream of study at higher secondary school.

2. There will be no significant difference in knowledge gain in terms of pre-post scores of the students according to the medium of instruction at school level.
3. There will be no significant difference in knowledge gain in terms of pre-post scores of the students according to the place of residence.
4. There will be no significant difference in knowledge gain in terms of pre-post scores of the students according to their inclination towards social science.
5. There will be no significant difference in knowledge gain in terms of pre-post scores of the students according to their family's legal exposure.
6. There will be no significant difference in knowledge gain in terms of pre-post scores of the students according to the social work background.
7. There will be no significant difference in knowledge gain in terms of pre-post scores of the students according to their mother's occupation.
8. There will be no significant difference in knowledge gain in terms of pre-post scores of the students according to their exposure to TV and video.
9. There will be no significant difference in knowledge gain in terms of pre-post scores of the students according to the socio-economic status.
10. There will be no significant difference in knowledge gain in terms of pre-post scores of the students according to the overall modernity.
11. There will be no significant difference in knowledge gain in terms of pre-post scores of the students according to the their personality.
12. There will be no significant difference in knowledge gain in terms of pre-post scores of the students according to the level of academic achievement.
13. There will be no significant difference in knowledge gain in terms of pre-post scores of the students according to their English competence.

LIMITATIONS OF THE STUDY

The present study is limited to:

1. The study is limited to the first year Home Science students enrolled in the year 1992-93 in the Faculty of Home Science, M. S. University, Baroda.
2. The experiment is limited to teaching only selected units of the outline of the course "Women and Law".

Chapter 2

Review of Literature

Issues, concerns and welfare of women have gained momentum in our country. This has resulted in a spurt of print materials. Research organizations have come up to deal with topics concerning women. There is widespread media coverage and production of reports of Government of India and voluntary organizations monographs research papers, reports of seminars and conferences on "Women and Law".

While reviewing the literature available for this study, the investigator reviewed the previous work related to the present investigation by evaluating research reports, observations and opinions of different authors and also of theoretical papers published by social scientists from time to time. The law books dealing with various legal provisions for women, various articles in legal and social science periodicals were read from important reports such as reports of the Law Commission towards equality-report by the Committee on Status of Women (1988). The investigator found that no study has so far been conducted or no video film has been developed on "Women and Law." Therefore, in this chapter the investigator has reported those studies which are directly or somewhat related to the present study.

In this chapter an attempt has been made to conceptualise the theoretical as well as the empirical foundation of the present investigation as adequately as possible. A discussion on the conceptual foundation on the need for developing a course and producing video package on "Women and Law" has been presented. Empirical evidences gathered from various studies are reported and discussed under the following sections.

1. Conceptual foundation of giving Legal Education to women.
2. Empirical foundation of the need to provide Legal Education.
3. Empirical foundation of the course "Women and Law".
4. Empirical foundation of effectiveness of Educational Television.
5. Empirical foundation of the effectiveness of video films for teaching.
6. Brief resume of reviews and its relevance to the present investigation.

CONCEPTUAL FOUNDATION OF GIVING LEGAL EDUCATION TO WOMEN

Time and again, at seminars, workshops and meetings of women academics, activists and the public, the need for "legal education" is identified. In this section an attempt is made to discuss Various problems faced by women and the underlying factors responsible for these problems.

This part carries the findings, recommendations of various workshops, seminars and conferences and highlights the need to provide legal education to women.

The Asian Women Scholar's Seminar held in May, 1978 at Ewha Women's University, Seoul, Korea on "Role of the University in Women's Movement" made the following recommendations :

Women's consciousness must be developed according to the changing times. They must be informed of their legal rights, of, how they may seek redress and legal aid whenever needed. Social change is possible only by working with young generations. This can be done by raising women's consciousness and by developing a feminist perspective in all areas of academic discipline.

The Seminar on "Creative Women in Changing Societies" was held from 9th to 13th July, 1980 in Oslo, Norway, with the major objectives: (1) to identify the psychological and structural determinants that allow or prevent creativity in women and to explore the similarities and differences among creative women within the same professions in different cultures. (2) to discuss the ways in which contemporary political and other structures can be used effectively for the advancement of women and to examine alternative perspectives, structures and institutions.

Over 50 outstanding women and men from 20 countries from all regions of the world attended the Seminar. The Seminar recommended that–

Free and equal education should be given to both girls and boys. Research programs to identify and study barriers preventing the full participation of women in science and technology should be developed in order to determine effective strategies for reducing or eliminating these barriers. Because research and programs developed by men without the participation of women seldom involve consideration of women's concerns, men should be encouraged to concern themselves more actively with issues pertaining to women in their professional activities. Legislation prohibiting discrimination in employment and education and requiring affirmative action should be enacted.

This excellent example of efforts on behalf of women, to promote their access to decision making positions, should be followed by other United Nations Organizations.

A National Conference relating to women's studies organised in Trivendrum, in 1984, concluded that the problems of dowry can not be uprooted by legislation, alone; more stringent approaches tackling the issues at the grassroot level are needed. Further the implementation of the laws and discouraging the practice of dowry should be strengthened.

In the same Conference, while discussing the issue on Women and family law, it was pointed out that contrary to common belief, women's problems related with the family do not invariably arise out of the 'conflict' situations : instead, they often arise due to ignorance, unmethodical arrangements and procedural requirements. Further the Conference stated that Hindu women have not gained much from amended laws due to their ignorance of law, attitudinal inhibitions like fear of public opinion, unfamiliarity with formal cumbersome legal procedure and their incapacity to reach and use the legal procedure. The delegates pointed out that to make the innovative family laws a success, in improving the lot of Indian women, the procedural technicalities need to be reshaped, so that women are encouraged to take advantage of these laws. In addition, the women need to be educated to increase their awareness about their rightful claims.

Similar observations were made in a National Seminar on "Legal aid for Women-The Role of Voluntary Organizations" held in Delhi in 1986.

The participants in the Seminar were also of the view that women should be made aware of their legal rights to strengthen their position and enable them to seek promised relief under the laws. They stressed the need for propagating laws affecting women, on national media through imaginative programmes so that a larger percentage of the people are covered. In addition schools, colleges and in facts communities at large should be educated on criminal laws and social laws related to women.

A two-day Seminar on "Utilizing Law and Legal Processes for Women's Development" was held in Delhi, in 1987. It was organized in collaboration with the All India Women's Conference, Delhi Legal Aid and Advice Board and Crimes Against Women Cell of Delhi Police.

The Seminar made the following recommendations:

Audio-visual materials should be used to promote greater legal literacy. Women should understand law and legal procedures. There is great need to publicise the legal rights of women through radio, television and through formal and nonformal education system. The Department of Women and Child Development, Ministry of Human Resource Development,

Government of India, should include scheme for promoting legal literacy among women through active involvement of universities, colleges and voluntary organizations. Films should be produced showing various prejudices against women starting from female birth till the old age to spread legal literacy.

Asian Women's Conference on "Women, religion and family law" was held in Bombay, from December 16 to 20, 1987. The delegates came to the conclusion that the "one common source of continuing discrimination against women is the patriarchal nature of our societies and culture which is often strengthened and institutionalised by the unequal nature of family laws". The delegates expressed concern that in almost all the countries represented in the conference, with the exception of Singapore and Laos, the State has discriminated against women by encouraging fundamentalism and chauvinism. It was pointed out that all religions had one similarity in that none of them gave equal status to women. Religion was, in fact, being used as a weapon to "suppress" women.

The conference felt that in many countries that had espoused egalitarian ideology and theoretically held men and women to be equal, stuck to laws that effectively neglected this principle. The conference observed that the women's movement had effectively challenged many of the humiliating and unfair practices in the face of State repression, religious chauvinism and patriarchal dominance.

The Central Executive Committee (CEC), of the All India Democratic Women's Association (AIDWA) held its meeting on June 25, 1988 in Delhi. Representatives from 12 States attended the meeting. They have reported "Rape is increasingly being used as a 'class weapon" by landed interests with State backing against the increasing struggles of the rural poor". The Committee noted that India is first among all nations in custodian rape, according to a UN report.

The CEC strongly condemned the growing atrocities on rural poor. It called for a countrywide struggle against divisive, communal and casteist forces in support of all the Harijan and

Adivasi women. It called for joint struggle with different women's organisation's for national unity and against religious fundamentalist forces.

In a National seminar held in Patna in 1989 on "Women and Violence-various manifestations" the speakers highlighted several points, the major being: Illiteracy and lack of legal education of women due to which their existing situation had deteriorated. The need to make women aware of legal rights and procedures. The need for media to be geared to play a constructive and positive role in reporting the incidents of violence.

Seminar on "Women's Development and Legal Literacy" was organised by Department of Home Science, Amravati University on 18th and 19th January, 1990. The broad objectives of the seminar were to create awareness about the status of women and use of laws and legal processes for women's development. In all 83 participants - Resource persons, women teaching staff from local post graduate Teaching Department of Home Science of the University, participated and highlighted various problems of women and child education. Various laws such as Hindu Marriage Act, 1955, Custody of Children, Maintenance to wife, Adoption Act, etc. were discussed. Atrocities against women and problems of urban educated women were highlighted. Collective and sustained actions can bring the change in the attitude of the society. It recommended the need of women' s Development Programme and importance of "Legal Literacy" amongst women.

Mehta (1992) discussed Indian Penal Code Section 497 (Adultery) and Hindu Law (Inheritance) and highlighted the discrepancy in sex matters in Indian Laws. Mehta further discussed the reforms and changes done by Government of India in the laws. The only difficulty is about the implementation of legal protection given by Indian Laws due to lack of efficient witnesses and also lack of eagerness on the part of the complainant. Mehta emphasised importance of spreading the message of justice and equality among illiterate women as well as socially coward attitude of literate women.

The National Perspective Plan for Women 1988-2000 A.D., in the report of the core group set up by Department of Women and Child Development, Ministry of Human Resource Development, Government of India, 1988, revealed that the women in Indian society, have not fully realised the potential power that laws and legal processes hold for them in matters of development. They are ignorant of their own rights or are afraid or unable to enforce them due to expensive, complicated and long drawn out proceedings. Thus, they do not have easy access to justice. There is an urgent need for organised articulation, on the part of women and for all those who support women's development with equality and justice. This could be done by creating legal awareness amongst people and especially women, by making them aware of their legal rights.

Shah and Ojha (1990) in Baroda, reported that the social and cultural inhibitions against a woman in India are many. If women are left behind, progress will be slow. While discussing the need for legal awareness among women they commented that:

> "Since most men fear loss of control over women, they are not likely to free women and treat them with equality and justice on their own. The unjust treatment to women must be questioned by the women themselves. Education can help to create legal awareness among women. A number of women's studies centres have been established at the university level in our country. Based on their research findings, courses, such as "Women and Law" for college girls can be introduced in their core study programmes." (Shah and Ojha,1990, p. 32)

The legal education can be incorporated in the teaching programmes in the girls' colleges. There is need to spread legal education to the school drop-outs and illiterate girls and women in rural and urban poor areas. The non-formal educational media can develop legal awareness among them.

Shah and Ojha (1990) beautifully pinpointed the importance of legal education as:

> "Education can be an effective instrument of change only if it can help liberate women from oppressions and exploitations. Formal and non-formal education need to educate women and others about women's plights and the role legal awareness can play in emancipation of women."
>
> (Shah and Ojha,1990, p. 35)

Mittal (1992) observed that during the past two decades, women's issues are being increasingly added to the curriculum of undergraduate and post graduate courses of Indian universities.

The promotion of new knowledge about women in development should be viewed as an instrument of social change. Inclusion of Women's issues as an integral part of teaching curriculum in various disciplines is needed. Gender disparity and women's struggle is to be viewed as multidimensional social problems as a hindrance in building an egalitarian society.

In different disciplines of arts, humanities, social science, pure and applied science and commerce and management, themes pertaining to socio-cultural plurality, Indian political system with reference to women, marriage and divorce rights, power leadership, family land property, socio-cultural evils, law pertaining to women, can be suitably included to develop an educational system which is not sexist.

It could be inferred from the researches reviewed in this section that it is not enough to pass a law. There has to be a continuing education of the people of the purpose behind the Acts, so that they themselves can become the watchdogs of the laws. Therefore, during the past few years there has been greatly increasing awareness and interest in making women aware of the laws. The findings, recommendations of various workshops, seminars and conferences have highlighted the need for 'legal education' for women.

In 1984, 1986, 1989 and 1990 the need to educate women

about their rightful claims have been stressed. Whereas in 1989, 1990, 1992 trend changed and importance of audio-visual materials for promoting legal literacy was stressed. And for this purpose use of Radio and Television was suggested.

Recently in 1992 need for adding women's issues as an integral part of teaching curriculum in various disciplines is recommended. Thus, the investigator has developed course on "Women and Law" to fulfill this need. Spreading of legal education through formal and non-formal education system could help in removing legal unawreness among women.

EMPIRICAL FOUNDATION OF THE NEED TO PROVIDE LEGAL EDUCATION TO WOMEN

This part carries the articles providing statistics on crime against women, highlighting the need to provide Legal Education.

Hindustan Times, November 25, 1987 brought to the notice of the people that a record number of 1,319 dowry death cases were reported in 1986 as against 837 in the previous year, from various States. The Southern States recorded an upward trend. The figures rose from 13 to 79 in Andhra Pradesh, 35 to 54 in Karnataka and 12 to 38 in Tamil Nadu. Uttar Pradesh reported highest number of such cases -461 in 1986 and 323 in 1985.

According to Patriot, Bombay, January 12, 1988, more and more women are coming forward to seek redressal from the menace of dowry and related demands due to growing awareness of the social evil, according to women's organisations, social workers and police. These organisations have, however, decried the slow judicial process which has resulted in few or no convictions. They have also called for the establishment of special courts for speedy disposal of cases relating to dowry and harassment of women. In 1986 The Dowry Prohibition Act of 1961, was amended which has enhanced the minimum punishment to five years imprisonment and put the burden of proving that there was no demand for dowry on the accused, and the introduction of Sections 498-A relating to cruelty to a woman, and 304-B defining dowry deaths in the Indian Penal Code, have also helped women speak out on the issue.

The Centre for Social Research, New Delhi, which did an exhaustive study on dowry reported the number of deaths were astronomically higher than what was reported and that is true in other States as well. In Delhi, about 423 cases of deaths of married women were reported in the first six months of 1987, 300 of whom died of burns. In Bihar, according to reports, 6000 women died of burns in 1986 and in Bombay alone 1044 women died in 1985 and 991 in 1986. Forum Against Oppression of Women said the Government was trying to isolate the problem as a women's issue and was not recognising it as a form of violence against women.

The Times of India, November 19, 1989 reported by Rai that for years it was only the tribals; the dalits, and the women working in the fields who were subjected to sexual assaults. But now more women were working in the cities, and the rate of crimes against these women has also increased. In 1983, 5298 rape cases were registered throughout the country. In 1984 it rose to 6,203 and in 1985 to 6,356 cases, a 20 per cent increase in three years' period. The number of cases of molestation shot up from 11,814 in 1983 to 15,160 in 1985, a 28 per cent increase.

Hindustan Times, December 7, 1989 made a report that a majority of women in India were unaware of their rights. The Union Minister of State for Education and Culture Mrs.Krishna Shahi revealed the fact that although Government had passed progressively revolutionary laws to bring the women of the country at par with men, a lot still remained to be done. Quoting the Constitution, Mrs. Shahi said that in India many old laws regarding legal rights of women have been modified and new ones brought into force, specially during the UN Decade for Women (1976-1985). Yet the majority of women were unaware of their legal standings. Thus, emphasised the need for spread of legal literacy.

Vikasini (1989) reported that the atrocities against women is a world wide phenomenon. Some facts showing atrocities on women:

In the U.S.A. a rape is committed every six minutes. One in five women on an average is beaten or sexually harassed in West Germany. In India, rape is committed every 2 hours.

Every year there are around 4,000 rapes. Around 100 women and children every month are smuggled out of Bangladesh to be sold as prostitutes or as source material for organ transplants. Sale of young girls to old men in marriage is a common practice in Baluchistan and Pakistan. About one in five Australian adults believe that a man is justified in beating his wife. 22 per cent of Australian men and 17 per cent women believe that man has a right to kick, hit his wife if she disobeys him, refuses to sleep with him or admits to sleeping with another man.

Hindustan Times, August 12, 1989 showed the statistics on dowry deaths of married women which were alarming. Between 1986 and 1988 dowry deaths showed an increase of 65 per cent, rape increased by 9 per cent, molestation by 5 per cent and kidnapping by 44 per cent in the same period. It only goes to provide one point : laws, however, stringent are alone not an answer to checking these crimes.

The Times of India, Ahmedabad, March 9, 1990 reported women demand equal rights. Various women's organisations staged an impressive rally in the city under the banner of "Nari Ekta Manch" on the occassion of International Women's Day. Posters highlighting various problems faced by women and their struggle for equal status were displayed by the students of Communication Development Centre of Gujarat University. Various groups also presented skits and songs based on the theme of rights of women.

They also demanded the removal of all discriminatory laws, which accorded women a secondary status and also made them vulnerable. Women should be given equal rights within the family and must be entitled to equal share in property.

In view of the increasing number of dowry deaths, the Government should strictly implement anti-dowry laws, they demanded. The other demands included total prohibition, a ban on pre-natal sex determination tests, setting up women's co-operative banks in every district and action against makers of films, advertisements and literature degrading women.

Reviews of the articles and bulletins have established that the women are harassed, illtreated and crime against women is alarming. It can be concluded that the continuing-increase in the crime rate and worsening conditions of life of women in India (Figure 1). It is time to direct educational system to contribute towards improvement of women's status in India.

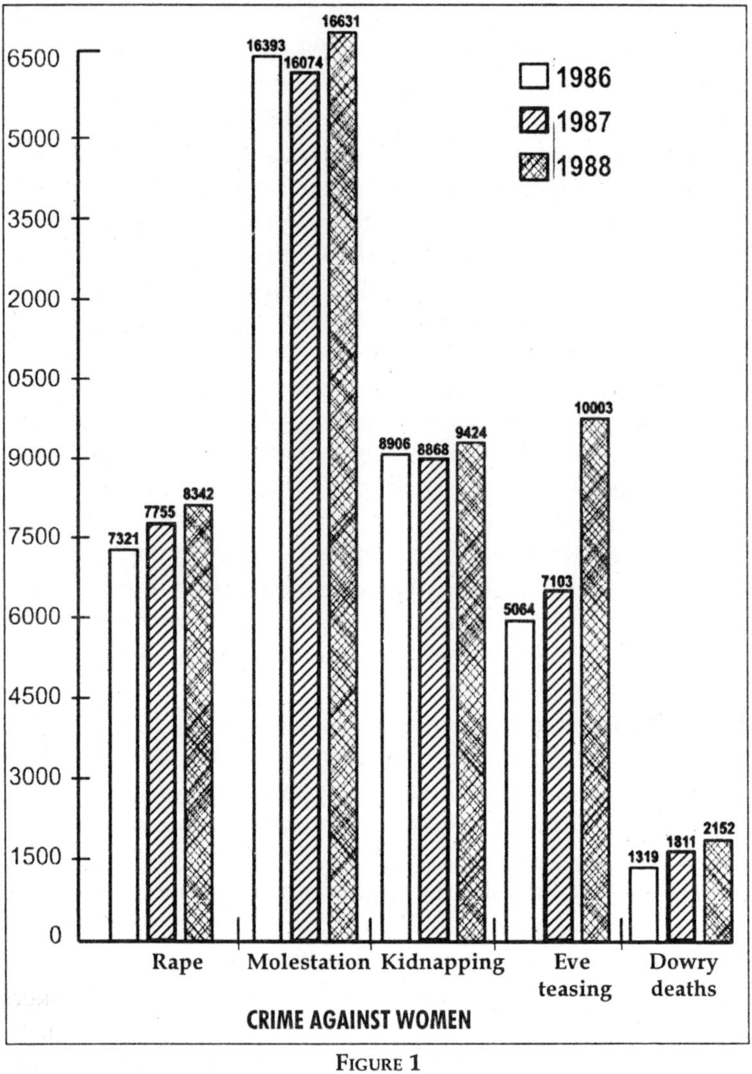

FIGURE 1

*Source: **Times of India*** Research Bureau, 1990

EMPIRICAL FOUNDATION OF THE COURSE "WOMEN AND LAW" FOR UNDERGRADUATE STUDENTS

The research evidences collected by the different researches in India and in foreign countries have highlighted the need to start the course on "Women and Law".

Research In India to Reflect the Need of the Course "Women and Law"

Sachidananda and Sinha in Bihar (1984) conducted a study to find out the awareness among men and women about legal rights. The population consisted of 960 male and 960 females in the age group of 18 to 50 years from Bihar.

The findings revealed that the bulk of rural and many of the urban women had not even heard of the existence of various laws. Ignorance was less pronounced among urban women and the numerical distribution revealed that women from Gaya were more aware than those from Bhagalpur, Madhubani and Ranchi. The right to inherit parental property was among the most known rights among women from rural as well as urban areas. Among the least known rights were those relating to Medical Termination of Pregnancy (MTP).

The women favoured laws for dowry, child marriages, widow remarriages. But other laws like MTP, property rights, divorce and law raising the age at marriage had not been favoured. Largest section of women had known the rights through family members, friends and neighbours.

Noted bulk of men from urban areas of the four cultural zones had revealed their willingness for granting equality to women. Rural men still considered women subservient to men. They were ignorant about the fact that women had been granted legal rights.

Majority of the rural men had revealed their liking for widow remarriage, dowry, equal wages and property rights. Urban men had disfavoured the laws of equal wages and MTP.

Dhagamwar in Maharashtra conducted a study in 1987 to find out the awareness of law amongst women and to find out the extent of the role of educational system in creating the awareness. Sample consisted of 65 women who came to the

Poona District Court, for relief under the Hindu Marriage Act during a five years (1973-1977) period.

Open ended questionnaires were used. The findings revealed that level of awareness among women was very poor regarding law. The element of ignorance was smaller with educated women. General awareness was lamentably lower age at marriage, regarding all aspects of law like minimum validity of polygamous marriage, grounds for divorce, etc.

The findings regarding the extent to which schools had anything to do with creating legal awareness among women, showed that schools seemed to do nothing to produce this awareness. Further schools did not counter or challenge the traditional upbringing the girls received in their homes.

Dhagamwar (1987) rightly suggests,

> "How far can the educational system, which has so far cast its weight behind the social norms be reshaped to create an atmosphere of equality, to instill the sense of being a human being first, and then a member of either sex? This in effect is the question we are asking when we ask what the educational system can do to create that legal awareness without which people do not resort to the laws to solve their problems."
>
> (Dhagamwar, 1987, p. 110)

Srivastava (1988) reported that several legal provisions have been passed for welfare of women, yet they continue to suffer. There is a big gap in the enactment of legal provisions and the benefits reaching to women. Lack of awareness of their rights and lack of knowledge of law is the reason why women continue to be mute victims of an unjust and irrational society.

Majority of the women in the country are still receiving humiliating, oppressive and sometimes very cruel treatment. There is need to create awareness in society and change people's attitudes towards women. More so, women themselves need to develop a self identity so that they can lead a life of security and dignity. This cannot be achieved without making her aware of her rights and potentials.

Bhoite (1988) reports in India equality of women seems to be insured by constitutional and legal measures. After independence the way seemed open for a change in the status of women and for an improvement in their standing in society. This study illustrates that this picture hides the continuing oppression of women in India. The major finding of the study is that, despite legal reforms since independence, the sex ratio has, in fact, continued to decline, indicating that these measures are far from adequate and obviously not applied. Bhoite"s major concern is that the world is not deceived by the false picture of sex equality in India.

Research in Foreign Countries, to Reflect the Need of the Course "Women and Law"

Jahan (1983) made these observations that in recent years, family violence has become an increasingly visible and important social issue in Bangladesh. Family violence directed against married women, is one of the most frequent but underreported crimes in the country.

In this context Jahan (1983) commented:

> "In Bangladesh, the male dominance of women in both public and private life has been reinforced by religious sanctions favouring men i.e. polygamy; men's right to divorce unilaterally; the son's right to inherit a double share of that of a daughter, etc. Purdah values, by segregating women and sanctioning strict gender based division of labour, have made women especially subservient and economically dependent on their male relatives."
>
> (Jahan 1983, p. 42)

The following factors are obstructing the social recognition of the problem. The male dominance of women in both public and private life has been reinforced by religious sanctions favouring men. The country wide poverty and scarcity of resources further limit women's access to opportunities for economic independence from families.

However, public awareness of such violence has recently increased quite sharply, because of the notorious 'dowry' deaths. Recent development in women's stand against violence as a result several seminars are organised to articulate their thoughts on violence and publicize their stand against violence, but there is need to carry out research studies on violence. Need for public education regarding women's rights and legal measures protecting them from infringement should be more emphasized. This can be done by introducing educational programs, based on simple pamphlets elucidating various aspects of laws and legal procedures protecting women's rights.

Hilary (1987) in Milton Keynes studied 129 legal cases and medical texts, psychiatric reports and found that a woman appearing before the criminal court is about twice as likely as a man, to be dealt with by psychiatric, rather than penal means. A woman is more likely to be found unfit to plead or insane. Hilary interviewed groups of professionals like lawyers, judges, probation officers and Psychiatrists. This is a detailed study which theorises how gender is interwoven into the discourses of law and medicine, revealing some profoundly worrying practices for women and men. She identified some of most uncomfortable practices on the interface of law and medicine. Woman should give up the benefits, as well as the disadvantages of feminity. Nonetheless the author remains committed to the principle of equality in the distribution of justice.

Shehla *et al* (1982) conducted a research study sponsored by Women's Division Cabinet Secretariat, Government of Pakistan, Islamabad. Titled "Muslim Family Laws and their implementation in Pakistan", with the major objective to gain an insight into the factors preventing or hindering Muslim women from exercising and obtaining their legal rights under the family laws and to make practical and feasible recommendations.

Sample consisted of 150 women from Lahore. Data were collected from two family courts, three Unions Councils at Lahore. The major findings were as follows:

Non maintenance by husband appeared to affect a majority of women. Majority of the divorced women do not agitate in the legal forum, mainly because they are unaware of their entitlement to maintenance. Maintenance is not claimed through the legal forum for the children by a majority of divorced women due to the fear of the children being taken away by the husband. Lengthy legal procedure is involved in the recovery of dowry and as such majority of women feels discouraged to dowry claim it as their legal right in the court of law. Women are willing to forgo a lot of rights and tolerate hardships rather than seek dissolution.

Recommendations made by Shehla *et al* were: Both, girls and boys, at college level should be taught course on "Women's Rights under Islamic Law". Elementary course on "The Rights of Women under the Family Laws" be included in Adult Educational Programmes. Cassette recording giving detailed information in rights of women in Urdu as well as in regional languages should be prepared. Regular programmes should be initiated on both television and radio concerning different aspects of women's right.

Barbro (1988) reported that in Sweden, as in most other Western countries, violence against women has become a public issue. Despite its historic occurance in virtually every time period of human existence, it has only recently been defined as a social 'problem' and not as a private affair. Most social programmes that deal with the problem are, therefore, quite recent so that little definitive evaluation of their impact is available as yet. This paper attempts to provide a short survey of the most important activities for countering violence against women that are currently ongoing in Sweden.

Dagg and Thompson (1988) made an inquiry on the nature and extent of sexism and sex discrimination in contemporary Canadian universities paints a familiarly depressing picture. Data drawn from official statistics, from a number of qualitative studies and from own experiences show women's disadvantage and oppression as staff, academics and students in all areas of university life.

The figures do not reveal regional, 'ethnic variations; most of the qualitative material is drawn from English speaking and Ontario Universities. The employment difficulties faced by women scientists; sexist curricula and pedagogy in humanities', social sciences courses; the position of traditionally 'feminine' subjects (home economics, library science, nursing) poor availability of integrated women's studies courses and the lack of adequate funding support for feminist research topics. Equal opportunities policies, where these exist nationally or at institutional level, have not moved beyond statements of (overt) intent. A harrowing catalogue of issues and incidents of sexual harassment and violence directed by men academics/ students against women academics, students forms the back-cloth to the whole account.

From the overview of the reviews presented it is clearly established that women suffer ill treatment and can not protect themselves from crime because of unawareness of laws. Atrocities on women is a common phenomenon all over the world.

From the earlier studies reviewed so far it was evident that need has been identified to teach women about law. Jahan (1983), need for public education regarding women's rights and legal measures protecting them by introducing course on "Women and Law", in educational institutions. Sachidanands and Singh (1984), found people are unaware about the law. Dhagamwar (1987), reported low level of legal awareness and educational system can play important role in creating the legal awareness. Srivastava (1988), stressed the need to create awareness in society and bring about change in people's attitude. Shehla et al suggested that that both,girls and boys, should be taught course on "Women's Rights". Cassettes recording giving detailed information about rights of women should be used to spread legal literacy.

Thus considerable evidences are present in the literature as researches are indicating unawareness of women regarding law on one hand and the need to introduce course on "Women and Law" in educational institution.

EMPIRICAL FOUNDATION OF EFFECTIVENESS OF EDUCATIONAL T.V.

This part carries the research studies concerning the empirical foundation of effectiveness of educational television.

Lampkin Emmett Coleridge (1976) studied the adolescent Television use as a possible socialisation agent in the Stanford University. Sample consisted of eight hundred and sixty one students from three school grades (7,9,11) with four racial ethnic sub-groups and two social status groups defined by the respondent's father's attained level of education. A questionnaire administered in classroom situation was used to obtain information (1) media use patterns and preference; (2) reasons for viewing TV, (3) perceptions of TV as it relates to real life experience, (4) programme preferences.

Assessment of social status influences suggested that education through high schools does not provide clear distinctions between socio-economic groups nor does it affect electronic media use. The overall results for electronic media use present a staggering picture. The average adolescent reports spending over eight hours each day with some form of media, at least four hours of which are used to watch TV. Racial ethnic analysis showed black adolescent to be predominant users of electronic media (11 hours per day), five hours of which are devoted to TV.

Hanrahan and Joseph (1981), carried out a study in Indiana University, to analyse the life style characteristics of viewers of selected television programmes. In study life style was defined as the measurement of people's activities, interests and opinions. This study employed life style data to find out the life style differences existed between heavy and light viewers of two television programmes (Movie and Police Programmes) and heavy viewers across these programme types; life style variables enhanced the above analysis when age and household income were separately controlled; life style profiles revealed patterns supporting the assertion that programmes choice is value expressive behaviour.

The data for the study were derived from the 1975 National Consumer Mail Panel of Market Facts (4750 adults).

The study by Hanrahan and Joseph (1981) found statistically significant differences between heavy and light viewers within programme types. For example, female heavy movie viewers were significantly more price conscious, home oriented and involved in their community than were the light viewing counterparts.

Males who frequently viewed police programmes, had more religious and moral values than the male heavy movie viewers. Such results occurred in analysing both the total male and female samples. They suggested that programme type audiences are not homogenous and life style data can enrich viewers portraits even when demography is controlled.

Cherian (1986), undertook an experimental study with the purposes-to find out the impact of TV in terms of knowledge of rural people in the fields of health and hygiene, nutrition and family planning programmes; to analyse the general content of selected health and hygiene, nutrition and family planning TV programmes.

The sample of the study consisted of 600 women and men from selected villages of the Kheda district of Gujarat. A field experiment having pre and post observations in the experimental and control group was used in the study.

A knowledge test, reaction scale, socio-economic status scale and instrument on content analysis were used to collect the data.

The findings of Cherian's study were as follows:

1. Rural women and men took interest in watching the TV programmes produced by PiJ T.V.
2. T.V. viewing helped women and men to gain significant amount of knowledge about green leafy vegetables, polio vaccination and laproscopy.
3. Gain in knowledge was more among women than men.
4. Socio-economic status and age of the respondents were not associated with the gain and retention in knowledge.

Mehta (1988), studied the use of television for higher education under the countrywide classroom project of U.G.C. in India. The study is based on review of both statistical and documentary data. It included opinions of media experts, university teachers, media critics and on debates in the educational circle in India.

While discussing the role of Television in Higher education Mehta (1988), writes:

> "Educational broadcasting is generally used for extension of experience; evidence as the basis of study; explanation meaning how things happen; motivation; empathy and flight of imagination by taking the students outside the four walls of the conventional classroom to show them the world outside. It stimulates practical activity, and relates simple demonstration and experiments to their wider application, by the synthesis of specialised resources of research, illustration and dramatised presentations." (Mehta, 1988, p. 26)

Mehta recommended:

Television teaching improves the quality of the teaching and learning. It helps the specialist teachers to affect larger groups than they could without the aid. It is essential to recruit production staff young and with a good education. Training for television must take into account the limited funds, equipment and facilities with which the staff must operate. Technology can carry out its full potential for education, only in so far as, educators embrace educational technology as a system and integrate a range of human and non human resources into the total educational process. Administrators, educationists and others involved in designing for the future must take into account the changing pattern and use of technological media.

Chopra (1989), conducted an 'Audience profile study' to know the facilities available in the Faculties of M.S. University of Baroda. Sample consisted of all the colleges and Faculties of higher education affiliated to the M.S. University of Baroda. A questionnaire was used to collect the data.

The findings revealed that:

Most of the Faculties/colleges had a colour television in one of their departments. The students and teachers watched the television programmes. Majority of the Faculties/colleges had enough space for T.V. viewing. Programme Schedule of University Grants Commission was not received by any Faculty. Almost all the Faculties/colleges had some or the other audio-visual facilities.

Mehta, Desai and Shanaa (1989) carried out a study with the major objective to find out the overall effectiveness of the U.G.C. programme, "Invisible Work", on students of arts and commerce college of Idar, Gujarat.

Thirty students from arts and commerce college of Idar formed the sample of the study.

Findings revealed high majority of the respondents could understand the graphic/posters presented in the programme. Nearly equal number of the respondents found the amount of information to be too little and just enough, on the other hand ten per cent found it to too much. However, majority of the students found the language of the programme to be difficult to understand.

Seth (1983), conducted a study to check the effectiveness of educational television on the educational development of primary school children. The main aim of the research was to study the effectiveness of educational television, on the educational development of primary school children in terms of language development, acquisition of knowledge related to educational television programme, and scholastic achievements. In Seth's study the sample of 40 primary schools in Delhi, which were having television was selected as experimental group and the sample of 40 primary schools which were not having television were selected as control group. Intelligence tests and test of language development were used for collecting the relevant data.

Shastri (1990), from EMRC, Gujarat University carried out a Case Study - "Visual Profile of Countrywide Classroom".

Its objective was to assess the overall effectiveness of the 'Countrywide Classroom' programmes for the undergraduate students and to find out whether there was any benefit from the U.G.C. INSAT telecast. The R.R. Lalan College of Bhuj, was selected for the case study. The programme emphasised proper educational infrastructure and facilities available for the students in the college. The programme also consisted of interviews of the students and professors, reflecting their views and opinions about the countrywide classroom programmes. A group discussion was conducted in order to know the views of the students. Sample consisted of post graduate students of Gujarat University.

Findings and conclusions made by Shastri were : The programme was appreciated by most of the viewers. The programme throws light on two sides of the U.G.C.-INSAT telecast. On one side it reflects the difficulties of the students in taking the full advantage of the countrywide classroom programmes, like: unsuitability of time, English language, more emphasis on science subjects, etc.

On the other side it shows the reach of the countrywide classroom programmes in remote areas and its effectiveness. More programmes of this kind should be made. So that, the policy makers, people involved in production, producers, content experts, script writers etc. became aware of the changes which are needed to make the U.G.C. telecast more effective and useful.

It can be summarised from the earlier studies reviewed so far that many researches have been conducted to find out the effectiveness of educational T.V. Lampkin (1976), Hanrahan and Joseph (1981), studied the characteristics of viewers of television and hours of viewing.

Cherian (1988), and Seth (1983), carried out an experimental study whereas Mehta (1988), Chopra (1989), Mehta and Sharma (1989), conducted survey to study the effectiveness of educational T.V.

Lampkin (1976), and Seth (1983), used school students as sample whereas many researchers Hanrahan and Josephy (1981), Mehta and Sharma (1989), Mehta (1981), EMRC (1990), Chopra (1989), studied college students as sample.

Only Cherian (1986), carried out study with rural sample.

Both Lampkin (1976), and Cherian (1986), found SES not significantly associated with learning through educational T.V.

Only one study by Chopra (1989), studied the facilities in college for educational T.V. whereas Mehta (1989), Mehta and Sharma (1988), Cherian (1989), did content analysis of educational programme.

From the aforesaid discussions and reviews of various literatures, it was clear that number of researchers have established effectiveness of educational T.V. which is an inbuilt advantage of Audio Visual aids. Thus, the investigator was motivated to take up a research in this area, so as to get a better insight of effectiveness of video films to teach course "Women and Law" to Home Science students. Because, there was a dearth of research data pertaining to the use of video for teaching college students which the present study is taking care of.

EMPIRICAL FOUNDATION OF THE EFFECTIVENESS OF VIDEO FILMS FOR TEACHING

In the present study video has been selected as the components for the experiment. While reviewing the studies on video, it was found that many of studies have been conducted to find the effectiveness of the video.

A few significant researches can be cited here to throw light on the potential of video.

Staton (1979), attempted to investigate comparative effectiveness of two messages (simple and complex) and three media conditions (audio, written and video) for facilitating information gain in learning. 90 undergraduates were randomly assigned to six conditions. Each treatment group received a complex or a simple message transmitted by audio cassettes, audio-visual cassette or written study sheet. A two factor analysis of variance indicated a significant effect for media and not for the messages. Scheffe tests were performed to compare audio and video, video and written, written and audio media for both simple and complex messages. It was found that video wag more effective than audio in the retention of simple information. No difference was found between the complex audio message and complex video message. The simple video message was not found effective than the simple written message. Written is more effective, than audio in the retention of simple information. No difference was found between the complex written message and the complex audio message.

Hendrix (1980), conducted an inquiry to evaluate the contribution of the video tape self viewing, role playing and counsellor feed back in learning job interview skill in Oregon. With the aim of determining the effectiveness of video tape self viewing when used alone and with role playing and with counsellor feed back in teaching job interview skills.

The sample consisted of 28 graduate and undergraduate students at the University of Oregon, U.S.A.

All students attended three video taped sessions, which consisted of either (1) role playing only, or (2) role playing plus self viewing, or (3) role playing plus self viewing plus counsellor feed back.

Findings of the study revealed that self viewing subjects improved less than either role playing or counsellor feed back subjects. Self viewing when combined with role playing without the benefit of counsellor feed back resulted in less improvement than role playing alone. Degree of social anxiety across the groups affected perceived skill levels and self confidence but was not reflected in performance. Overall video tape self viewing were found to be effective.

Goswami (1986), undertook a study on video utilization by selected homemakers of Baroda city and their opinions regarding impact of video on family life, with the major objectives to study were. The video utilization pattern of the selected homemakers of Baroda city. The impact of video as an enhancer or an obstacle on family life.

The sample of the study comprised of 125 families of Baroda city. Interview cum questionnaire method was used for data collection. The findings of the Goswami's study revealed that-More than 90 per cent of the respondents bought video in their family to have recreation at their own convenience. There was high percentage of home makers having the impact of video as an enhancer in performing the social activities.

It was concluded that an effective, imaginative and carefully directed video viewing could help in developing a climate of acceptance, of video as a medium of information, education and entertainment.

Chandra, Shah, and Thomas (1987), conducted a study on the effectiveness of video cassettes, in imparting family centered knowledge upon a selected sample of women and adolescent girls from rural and urban areas. The purpose of the study was to find out : The knowledge gain of urban and rural women and adolescent girls, when instructed through video films, on conservation and purification of water. Change in opinions, if any, of urban and rural women and adolescent girls when exposed to the video films. Effectiveness of the video films using two approaches, that is, persuasive and informative approach.

In Chandra, Shah, Thomas (1987) study, a sample of 200 women and 200 adolescent girls was selected from urban area and 84 women and 84 adolescent girls was selected from rural area. A pre-test and post-test design was used to find out the knowledge gain and change in the opinions of the sample. The 't' test of statistical significance for dependent and independent variables was used to find out the pre and post difference in knowledge gain and change in the opinions through informative and persuasive approach of the video.

Through this study, Chandra, Shah, and Thomas, found out that majority of the respondents could improve their post test scores of knowledge significantly after viewing the films. The informative approach of video was more effective in improving the knowledge. The video films were not effective in changing the opinions of the sample positively.

Laul (1989), made study on comparison of video cassettes alone and along with handouts to teach adequate nutrition at low cost. Major objective of the study was to check the suitability of video cassettes for knowledge gain and practice change.

The sample consisted of 224 students of the VIth standard from Lai Bahadur Shastri School, Harni Road, Baroda.

Laul found that-All the respondents gained knowledge after viewing the video cassettes. Both persuasive and informative video cassettes were found to be effective for the knowledge gain of students regarding adequate nutrition at low cost.

Gupta (1990), studied the effectiveness of video films in terms of knowledge gain, on conservation and purification of water with VIth standard pupils from one urban school and one rural school of Baroda. The sample consisted of 150 students of IVth standard. All the students belonged to lower socio economic status and were between the age group of 9-12 years.

A questionnaire of knowledge test was used in pretest and posttest. The research design used was experimental of before and after type. Opinions of teachers regarding the video films as one of the teaching media were also collected.

Gupta noted that-The informative and persuasive video films were almost equally effective in teaching the content of conservation and purification of water. Rural students learnt more than the urban students through both the video films. The teachers were also interested in teaching their students through video films. They thought that through the video films more content can be taught in a shorter period of time and students can learn effectively through the video film.

Gupta (1990), conducted a study with the aim of producing a video film on selected voluntary organisations of Baroda and of validating the film in terms of the effectiveness in imparting information.

The sample consisted of 50 women from low socio economic status from police head quarters, Baroda. Gupta came to the following conclusions:

The film was found highly effective in imparting information regarding voluntary organisations working for women in Baroda.

Majority of the respondents liked the film. Film was found suitable to the following categories of the respondents:

- Younger and older age group.
- Low and high educational level group.
- Small and large family size group.

Gupta (1991), conducted a study with the objectives of producing a video film on "Puppetry" to instruct the Home

Science college students and testing its effectiveness in terms of gain in knowledge. The sample comprised of two categories of respondents, consisting of 55 undergraduate students of Department of Education and Extension and 8 teachers of the Faculty of Home Science.

Gupta reported the following findings:

The highly significant difference in the pretest and post test mean scores confirmed the effectiveness of the film. All the respondents in high and low familiarity with puppets as well as more and less exposure to T.V. and video. Majority of the respondents reported the video film having understandable and enough information, understandable language with interesting, clear and understandable visuals.

Mandal (1992), carried out a comparative study of the effectiveness of three instructional strategies in teaching selected aspects of puppetry to Home Science students of the M.S. University, Baroda. With the major objective of studying effectiveness of three instructional strategies in teaching puppetry and helping students in developing ability in making glove puppets. Sample comprised of 177 first year students, who were present for all the three classes (pretest, posttest and practicals).

Major findings of Mandal's study were as follows:

The gain in knowledge was more in lecture cum live demonstration and video film as compared to that of booklet. However, there was considerable gain in knowledge as well as development of ability in all the three experimental groups.

Overview of researches have shown that the studies on comparison of video film with other teaching aids are many in number. However, number of researches including use of video to college students are not substantial. Many research studies had used the experimental design to find out the effectiveness of video film.

BRIEF RESUME OF REVIEWS AND THEIR RELEVANCE TO THE PRESENT INVESTIGATION

Overview of the research highlighted the fact that laws have been amended to make the legal situation more favourable for women. Stringent laws have been passed to fight the growing crime rate. Unfortunately, all these amendments in law have yet to filter down to women's lives, in practice. One of the reason for this is that the women have been more or less passive spectators in influencing legal processes. Even where legislation exists and could be used to their advantage, a vast majority of women are ignorant of its existence or are not in a position to have it enforced in view of its inherent complexities. The result is that the law remains an ineffective instrument of social change.

No matter how big or good amendments were made, women continue to suffer because of ignorance and unawareness. Thus the investigator was motivated to make a course on "Women and Law" to teach girl students the various, simplified content related to laws.

It was further found that video being effective medium as it can teach even the theoretical content with variety. However, there was a dearth of studies on developing video package on "Women and Law".

Variables like exposure to TV/video, SES, medium of instruction which showed significance in some reviews are also presented in this investigation. All the researches agree on one point that there is need to educate women about law.

CONCLUSION FROM REVIEWS

1. Reviews of the studies conducted established that awareness of women regarding laws is very poor.
2. It was further revealed that a change was creeping slowly and steadily in policies of Government, women's organisations and need to spread legal education is felt.
3. More recently, renewed attention is being given to the inclusion of legal education in formal education system.
4. Reviews have shown rise in statistics on crime against women.
5. A sizeable theoretical literature was available on effectiveness of T.V. and video but very limited literature was found on teaching college students through video.

There is a need to develop systematic video film on "Women and Law". The amount of investigation, research on video film is limited which necessitated further exploration in this area. It is established that the law related course are strongly recommended for women.

Though need to educate women about law is felt, but trying out has not been done. Therefore, undertaking a study to develop the content of "Women and Law" to teach Home Science students assumes significance and should be given top priority.

Thus, it is obvious that course "Women and Law" can play a catalytic role in bringing about social change which is also the ultimate aim of Home Science education.

No study was available on teaching "Women and Law" hence, it is felt that teaching of law is perhaps completely neglected. Todays need is to restructure the curriculum keeping in mind the change. It was further found that the video being an effective medium, as, it can teach even the theoretical content with variety, however, there was still a dearth of studies on developing video package on "Women and Law".

From the overview of the review presented above, it was clear that there was a dearth of research studies pertaining to the development of course "Women and Law". Thus, the investigator was motivated to take up this study. The effectiveness of video film for teaching have been established. Thus, it was further thought to produce different video films to teach the content on "Women and Law", to the Home Science college students.

Chapter 3

Methods of Procedure

This chapter deals with the research procedure adopted for the present investigation. The present investigation aims at developing a course and a video instructional package on "Women and Law" and measuring the effectiveness of package with the students of Faculty of Home Science, Baroda.

The very nature of investigation necessitated undertaking multidimensional study revolving around those aspects of "Women and Law", which were not investigated in the past. The study was carried out using content analysis, experimentation and survey methods.

Developing course, producing video films, experimentation with the video films on "Women and Law", formed the nucleus of the study.

The chapter is discussed under the following sections:

1. Feasibility study
2. Population of the study
3. Operational definitions
4. Variables and their relationships
5. Model of curriculum planning
6. Preparation of scripts
7. Preparation of video films
8. Research tools
9. Validation of the research tools

10. Planning for experiment
11. Data collection
12. Conducting the experiment
13. Scoring and categorization
14. Analysis of data

FEASIBILITY STUDY

The investigator conducted a feasibility 1990 in the Faculty of Home Science, M.S. University, Baroda. Sixty First Year students were selected in such a way that there were twenty students, each representing Arts, Commerce, Science streams. Such a selection permitted a comparison between the awareness of students regarding laws pertaining to women and enabled the investigator to know whether the type of school education and characteristics of the students affected the awareness and opinions of the students.

The purpose of the feasibility study was to find out the data on background information of the students, source of legal information, their opinion about legal education being given to the girls and the correct knowledge about laws related to women like age for marriage, divorce, dowry, rape, eve teasing, inheritance, maintenance, etc.

It was intended that the findings of the feasibility study will help the investigator to crystalize her problem, to determine the feasibility of the doctoral study, to draw a meaningful sample and to select the relevant variables.

The data were collected with the help of questionnaire.

Implication of the Findings of Feasibility Study for the Present Study

The feasibility study showed that there was a lack of awareness among Home Science students regarding laws related to women. Findings showed that there were only 30 per cent girls who had correct awareness of the different laws concerning women. The remaining 70 per cent did not have any awareness or had incorrect awareness. This implies that corrective measures need to be taken and education on this aspect need to be provided.

The feasibility study also supported the need for legal education to be given to Home Science students because only 10 per cent of the respondents have had formal legal education and rest had never been offered a course on legal education in either school or college.

An encouraging observation of the feasibility study was that the girls had very favourable opinions about the need for imparting legal education. Thus, if a course on "Women and Law" is initiated it would be well received.

The variability of different characteristics of Home Science students confirmed certain assumptions and helped the investigator to formulate hypotheses like relationship between personal and demographic variables with awareness regarding laws and opinions about legal education to be given to Home science students.

POPULATION OF THE STUDY

The population of the present experimental study consisted of 306 First Year students of the Faculty of Home Science, M.S. University of Baroda in the year 1992-93. However, in reality only 279 students were attending the classes and the others dropped out. In other words, the population consisted of 279 students.

Sample

The following summary shows the number of student viewers and absentees for each video film.

Summary of numbers of viewers and absentees for seven video films.

Video Film	*Class Strength*	*Viewers*		*Absentees*	
	N	*f*	%	*f*	%
Introduction	279	207	74.2	72	25.8
Eve Teasing	279	225	90.6	54	19.4-
Inheritance	279	184	65.9	95	34.1
Marriage	279	217	77.8	62	22.2
Dowry	279	237	84.9	42	15.1
Divorce	279	233	83.5	46	16.5
Rape	279	215	77.1	64	22.9

It was decided to let the whole class of the 1st year view all the seven video films. But as the whole population did not remain present to view the video films, selective samples were only available for each video film instead of the population. Upon checking the attendance at the viewing of each film it was found that some students were absent at each viewing. Therefore, the numbers of viewers and absentees is presented in the summary. 306 students paid the fees in the Faculty office, but only 279 students attended the classes. From the total number of 279, different number of students were absent at the viewing of the video films. Thus, the selective samples for each video film had different number, as shown in the summary.

OPERATIONAL DEFINITIONS

Effectiveness

Effectiveness is the actual gain in legal awareness of the respondents, it is denoted by the difference between pre and post scores obtained by the respondents on a test regarding legal awareness.

Previous Academic Achievement

It refers to the percentage of the marks achieved in the Board examination of twelth standard.

Extroversion

People with this personality trait are socially adaptable like to co-operate and work with others, and are carefree in nature.

Introversion

People with this kind of personality are shy, timid, inflexible, like to work alone and have tendency of worrying.

Ambiversion

People with this kind of personality have mixed characte-ristics of extroverts and introverts i.e. low extroversion and low introversion.

Women and Law

This course "Women and Law" will deal with laws concerning women, particularly laws related to eve teasing, dowry, divorce, inheritance, marriage, and rape.

Video Instructional Package

A set of seven video films of 12-30 minutes each giving information on laws related to women made by the investigator. Each covering a single unit of the course "Women and Law".

VARIABLES AND THEIR RELATIONSHIP

Social Work Background of Respondents

It is commonly presumed that environment at home affects individual's personality. In other words, it exerts impact on the mental horizon of the person. His or her world view is shaped to some extent by the background at home. Students coming from families having social work background may or may not differ from the students who do not have any social work background at home.

Type of Personality

The behaviour of the students is likely to be governed by their personality. Thus, there may exist some type of relationship between student's personality and their learning about "Women and Law", through video film.

Students who are shy, timid or introvert may find the video films novel and may learn with interest. The students whose personalities are extrovert, socially adaptable, outgoing, and carefree in nature will learn through video films as they will be motivated to learn more about laws.

So the type of personality may be associated with the gain in knowledge which is directly related to the effectiveness of the video films. Thus, the investigator wanted to find out the gain in knowledge or there may be no increase their knowledge.

Thus, exposure to television and video may have relationship with the gain in knowledge directly imparted by the video film. Thus, the investigator wanted to find out the effectiveness of the video films, if any, with the students having different level of exposure to television and video.

Modernity

The women of today, seek equality in all spheres of life, seeking and getting this equality depends on their own values, mental framework, familial and social context in which they, function. Students in First Year Home Science are heterogeneous in their level of modernity.

Students who are modern may gain high knowledge on "Women and Law". As the content may be in their line of thinking and thus get motivated to see video film and gain high knowledge through it. Whereas, the students who are traditional may find the content very different and novel. To them also video film may be interesting.

So, the modernity may be associated with the gain in knowledge which is directly related to the effectiveness of the video films. Thus, the investigator wanted to find out effectiveness of the video films, if any, with the student having different levels of modernity.

Mother's Occupation

Mother's participation in the world of work may bring about structural and functional alterations in the family. Mother's employment status may have relationship as far as the learning of course "Women and Law" is concerned. This may be due to the fact that women play a pivotal force in every family. They shape the family and inculcate habits in their children. It has been known that education of mother means education of the family. If a mother is educated/employed and aware of her rights and duties, she will transmit that awareness to the family members more easily. So, it would be interesting to study the effectiveness of the video films with the students having employed mothers in comparison to the students having mothers working as housewife.

English Competence

The students in First Year Home Science came from different schools having different medium of instruction. So, the students coming from different background vary in their level of competence in English. If a student is unable to read, write and comprehend well in English, then she will not make appropriate progress.

The medium of instruction at Faculty of Home science, M.S. University is English. Effectiveness of the video films would depend on how well a student can understand the language. Thus, it will be interesting to know if variations in the levels of competence in English has any relationship with the effectiveness of the video films in terms of gain in knowledge.

Stream of Study at Higher Secondary School Level

Students from different background are admitted to the First Year Home Science. The respondents who had offered Arts/ Commerce/Science or Home Science at school, may differ in their learning about "Women and Law" through video films.

The different background influence student's habits of studying, ways of thinking and learning the content taught. Thus, it was felt important to check the relationship between students' stream at higher secondary level and gain in knowledge which is directly related to effectiveness of the video films, if any, with the students having different, stream of study at Higher secondary school level.

Legal Exposure

It is well known fact that environment at home affects individuals' personality, students coming from such families where parents are in legal profession or any family member being involved in any kind of legal procedures, this kind of exposure may affect the mental make up of the students. They may be more motivated to learn laws as they may be little more familiar to the procedure and terminology of laws in comparison to those students who do not have any legal exposure. Thus, there may exist some type of relationship between students with legal exposure and without legal exposure and their learning about "Women and Law" through video film.

Medium of Instruction at School

Students from different medium of instruction are admitted to the First Year Home Science. The respondents who had their schooling from English medium may or may not differ in their learning about "Women and Law", through video films, which are mainly in English.

Thus, the medium of instruction may be associated with the gain in knowledge which is directly related to the effectiveness of the video films, if any, with the students from different medium of instruction at school.

Social Science Inclination

In the Faculty of Home Science there are five departments offering five majors. All these major have varied nature of courses and learning experiences. Therefore, it was of interest to find out whether inclination towards these different majors made any difference in the learning of laws related to women.

Students who possess science inclination generally have interest in the scientific details, procedure and principles. At the same time students having social science inclination show interest in people human relation and possess humanistic interest, that is, they like to deal with human relation and work with people.

So, the type of inclination may be associated with the gain in knowledge regarding "Women and Law". Thus, the investigator wanted to find out the effectiveness of the video films, if any, with the students having different type of inclination.

Place of Residence

In India 80 per cent of the population resides in 568,000 villages (Mehta 1988, p. 8). Girls' education is free in Gujarat it's result may be more parents are sending their daughters to schools and colleges irrespective of place of residence. Crime rate is more in cities in comparison to villages, respondents from cities may be more motivated to learn the content on "Women and Law". On the other hand the boundaries of cities are expanding and life in rural areas are influenced by life of cities to a great extent due to increased communication facilities and exposure to mass media.

So, the respondents from rural area may or may not be different from urban area. It was decided to select this variable as to know which group urban or rural will learn better the content on "Women and Law" through video films.

MODEL OF CURRICULUM PLANNING

This study is in the area of curriculum development and methods of teaching in the area of "Women and Law". There are several models of curriculum planning and development given by various authors. There are some major steps which are more or less being found in all the models.

Following a model ensured that all necessary and available facts were taken into consideration while planning the course. Because of this reason, the investigator followed a model for curriculum development suggested by Chandra, Shah and Joshi (1989).

This model is being adopted for the development of the course on "Women and Law". It has four parts which are in fact the steps to be followed in planning the course.

Model of Curriculum Planning

Consideration of Curriculum Needs

↓

Tentative Curriculum

↓

Try-out of Tentative Curriculum

↓

Evaluation of tentative Curriculum

Consideration of Course Needs

The investigator reviewed the literature in the form of reports of the Government of India, Seminar and Workshop reports, research reports, books, journals and newspaper articles. All these confirmed the fact that there are various laws for the benefit of women but because of lack of awareness among women regarding these laws, they are victimised.

The general observation and practical experience of the investigator is that the legal knowledge and awareness among Home Science students is poor.

Apart from the above mentioned reasons the investigator had observed that the students at the time of joining the Faculty of Home Science have a concept that this course would prepare them for good homemaking and vocations related to their fields. But very important part of life the legal aspect, is not taken care of.

The general observation and practical experience of the investigator is that this type of course would develop interest in the students towards the legal aspects of the life. Therefore the need was felt to teach this course through a video instructional package to create and sustain students' interest in the course and help them gain optimum knowledge.

Tentative Course

The second part of the model is to make tentative course which should include the educational objectives and learning experiences. Along with this information about the text and teaching aids were decided. Reading and reviewing of literature gave an insight to the investigator about the broad outline in which the investigator planned the course. The aim of this course was to create awareness and understanding among the students regarding laws concerning women.

Selection of Content

The first step of the investigation was to select the subject matter on laws related to women. Since there was no separate course on "Women and Law", which was offered by Faculty of Home Science, M. S. University, Baroda. The outline of the legal education and laws related to women were considered as bases to develop a course "Women and Law", for Home Science students. (Appendix-I)

The subject matter was selected from different sources like law books, journals and Indian Penal Code. The investigator selected the subject matter on law related to women and laws which were least known by the students were selected for making video. Thus, a cohesive mass of information dealing with laws related to women were selected.

In all, 5 libraries were referred they were Smt. H.M. Library, CASE Library (Baroda), Women Studies Center (Delhi), Women Studies Center (Baroda), ISRO (Ahmedabad) and EMRC (Ahmedabad). (Appendix–II).

The content for the course was divided under the following topics:

1. Introduction to law
2. Eve teasing
3. Marriage
4. Dowry
5. Inheritance
6. Divorce and maintenance
7. Rape

Organization of the Course

For better organization of the course the subject matter was divided into several units. Each unit containing major ideas and specific objectives. The concepts were arranged logically and proceeded from simple to complex. Each unit emphasizing only single topical dimension of the content.

Selection of Learning Experience

Appropriate learning experiences were decided, mainly classroom teaching through video films.

The format of the video films consisted of lecture from experts on legal aspects, presentation of case studies, and, dramatization.

Mode of Evaluation

For the measurement of the knowledge of the respondents about the various laws related to women, knowledge tests were developed. Questions were framed on the basis of the content of video films.

Developing the Course On "Women and Law"

The outline of the course "Women and Law" was developed on the basis of content analysis of the related course which were offered in Faculty of Home Science. The courses which were referred were "Marriage and family life" and "Laws and Family". Although these two courses were offered but they did not touch all the important areas of laws specially related to women. Secondly, the laws which were least known by the Home Science students during feasibility study were highlighted in developing the course "Women and Law". The findings of the study also helped in developing the course. Thirdly, the investigator consulted and took guidance from lawyers who were more or less conversant with the Home Science programme. Fourthly, the investigator discussed the content of the course with the Home Science teachers.

Thus, care was taken to develop a relevant and suitable outline in light of broad objectives of Home Science education.

Content Validation

The content as well as the developed course outline on "Women and Law" was judged by 11 experts from the fields of evaluation, curriculum and law. Five of them were teaching in Faculty of Home Science, 3 in Faculty of Law, M.S. University, Baroda, and 3 were practicing lawyers in Baroda. This team of experts judged the outline for the coverage of content, organization of the topics and suitability of the objectives with reference to the interest and comprehension of the undergraduate Home Science students.

In accordance with the suggestion of the experts a few changes were made in the organization of the topics and a unit on "Law of inheritance" was incorporated in the outline. Other suggestions were to use some simple words and to discuss real life cases for learning experience.

After making necessary changes in the outline of the course, it was checked by all the experts again and was finally approved by all of them.

Tryout of Tentative Course

During the tryout of the tentative course "Women and Law" the investigator tried to check the effectiveness of the developed course as well as the video package as a medium to teach laws to First Year Home Science students. The trial of the tentative course was most important and elaborate stage for this research. For trying out this course, the investigator actually conducted the experiments with the First Year students of Home Science.

Evaluation of Tentative Course

Evaluation is essentially to find out the extent to which the educational objectives have been achieved. To check for positive changes in the students' behaviour as a result of teaching this course.

The evaluations were done by conducting knowledge tests before and after teaching the course "Women and Law". If the evaluation shows that knowledge of the students had increased, then this course and the video films which were planned systematically by following a model, were good.

PREPARATION OF SCRIPTS FOR VIDEOS

The following steps were used to develop scripts.

(a) Knowing the subject gathered all the materials, met people, went to libraries, read newspapers. Reviews on relevant documents were done. Materials were collected widely.

(b) Arranging the sentence packets as logically as possible going from familier to unfamiliar. Ending with appropriate conclusion.

(c) Rewriting and necessary polishing was done to give the final product unity, proportion and continuity.

(d) The drafting of the full length scripts with a complete list of visual illustrations and accompanying sound.

Steps in Preparing the Script

The following steps were followed in preparing the scripts.

1. Descriptive type of commentary was written for seven video films on Introduction to law and Law for Eve teasing, Dowry, Divorce, Marriage, Rape and Inheritance.
2. The descriptive commentary was transferred into the format of script for video films for which these three steps were followed.
   (i) Developing written content.
   (ii) Developing visual content.
   (iii) Approval from media expert.

Developing Written Content

The content was written with necessary headings and captions. An effort was made to use, understandable words. All the major and important points were summarised at the end of each paragraph. Scripts for seven video films were written. As the films were to be informative, informative approach was used.

For two video films persuasive scripts were written. These were drama on marriage and dowry. The script for persuasive drama was written first in English. After finalizing, the script was converted into simple and understandable Gujrati. This was done keeping in mind the objectives, content organization, the physical appearance of the characters and scenes.

Developing Visual Content

After the scripts were written, the contents of the selected topics were transferred into form of visuals.

Visuals were made to be used for illustrative talk. Audio instruction, when presented with the use of visuals, it clarifies the concepts and leads to the meaningful association of ideas.

As far as the visual components were concerned, visuals/ graphics such as charts, flash cards, and diagrams were made.

Rough drafts having simple and uncluttered layouts were prepared. Then these sketches were given to the artist for preparing final drawings.

Charts and diagrams were prepared initially and the films with logical sequence were shot from the visuals.

Flash cards were made for emphasizing and summarizing major points of the topic.

Approval from Media Expert

After the scripts were ready, media experts from the ISRO, Ahmedabad, and EMRC, Ahmedabad were consulted for format organization, clarity of language and communicability.

The experts comments and suggestions were obtained. Certain changes were made on the basis of the comments of the experts. Thus, an effort was made to use simple understandable words.

Shooting Script

The shooting script was made by breaking down the screen play into shots by the investigator and taking care of the details of the technical aspects.

The shooting script was the blue print of the whole film. It gave the complete picture of the final schedule. It had all the details of camera direction, lighting suggestion, music and sound.

This is how the script was transferred into film form.

PREPARATION OF THE VIDEO FILMS

Preparation of video films were done in the following four separate stages.

1. Preproduction
2. Set up and rehearsal
3. Production
4. Post production

Pre-production

In pre-production stage the investigator decided about the cameraman and selected video camera (National 1000), two video cassettes, portable VCR, monitor, flash lights, stands, batteries, connecting wires, microphone, and equalizer for the production of the video films.

Set up and Rehearsal

(a) In this stage rehearsal of drama on marriage and dowry were supervised.

(b) Interviews were fixed with administrators, lawyers, social worker, a feminist, Dean of Faculty of Home science, and students of Faculty of Home Science.

(c) Took permission from the managing authorities for video shooting in hospital, Police station and Faculty of Home Science, all situated in Baroda.

Production

In this stage the actual shooting was done. Shooting was done by videographer, investigator and two helpers. The investigator had visualised the complete format of the video film and she discussed as an subject matter expert with the videographer who is a technical person. During the discussion she explained the scenes, angles and the points she wanted to be highlighted in the video films. Thus, she provided all the necessary tips. Handling of video camera and shooting was done by videographer. However, investigator was present throughout the shooting giving suggestions and directions to the videographer. The following steps were followed for actual shooting.

1. Making the required arrangements like making the required set ready and setting the camera according to the angles decided earlier.
2. Taking shots from the predecided angles. Taking shots included–
   (a) shots of the stills (graphics)
   (b) shots of the interviews
   (c) shots of drama
   (d) shots of commentator.

Post Production

The unedited shots, called rushes were viewed. In this stage the shots were screened. Some were without sound and some had only dialogues.

Then editing was done. In this stage mixing and editing was done. For mixing, recording or re-recording of sound was done, so as to blend the audio with visuals.

In editing, the film was cut to make the picture of the right length. This was done by taking the counts of each shots. Then the selected shots were transferred along with the titles on the other cassette.

At last, inserting and synchronizing of commentary was done and music was provided. Finally, the computer graphics were inserted for titling.

Thus, selecting, arranging and combining scenes and sound track were done to make the final films. It created the required flow, rhythm and tempo.

Previewing

This was advance showing of the films to the guide, investigator and videographer before it was shown to the formal group of students. This was done to judge the communicability of the film.

RESEARCH TOOLS

Construction of the Questionnaire

The questionnaire for collecting the information from the respondents for the present study was developed on the basis of feasibility study conducted by the investigator, review of literature from various books, journals and papers, personal experience of the investigator and also through discussion with her colleagues. The various sections of the questionnaire were developed according to the objectives. The detail description of each section of the questionnaire is present here.

Two different research tools were used for data collection. They were : (1) Questionnaire, and (2) Knowledge Test.

1. Questionnaire: Within the questionnaire it had four parts consisting:

Part 1: Background information-This part consisted of a checklist with structured response regarding the variables related to personal factors of the respondents. (Appendix–III).

Part 2: Scale for Socio-economic Status-This part consisted of a standardized socio-economic scale prepared by Desai (1987). (Appendix–IV).

Part 3: Scale for overall modernity-This part consisted of a scale to measure level of modernity of the respondents. The scale was adapted and standardized by Mehta *et al* (1974) from the original 'OM' scale of Modernity for Indian conditions. The original scale was prepared by Inkles and Smith (1974). (Appendix–V).

Part 4: Scale for personality-This part had a scale to measure the personality of the respondents. The personality inventory by A. Hafeez and V.S. Shantamani (1974) was used. (Appendix–VI).

Construction of Knowledge Test

Seven knowledge tests were prepared to measure the gain in knowledge. One test, for each of the seven videos was made. Knowledge tests involving recall and recognition items concerning laws related to women were constructed. True and false, fill in the blank and multiple choice questions were included in the test. Knowledge tests were used for pre and post tests in this experiment.

VALIDATION OF THE RESEARCH TOOLS

The research tools were given to different experts to find out its validity. The experts were from Faculty of Home science, Centre of Advanced Studies, (CASE), and Faculty of Law, all from the M.S. University of Baroda. The experts were asked to check the research tools regarding:

1. The coverage of content according to the objectives of the study,
2. Clarity or ambiguity in the use of language,
3. Format.

According to the experts' suggestions, necessary changes were made in terms of language and sentence formation.

The research tools which were ready for final data collection were pre-coded for easy coding and quick feeding into the computer for analysis. The knowledge tests were printed in five different colours, each for different laws. The idea of using different colours in the knowledge tests was to help the respondents in breaking the monotony of taking the knowledge tests.

PLANNING FOR EXPERIMENT

The experimental treatment were assigned to the classes rather than to the individual due to the ease of administration. Thus, the nature of the study was quasi experiment which took into consideration heterogeneity of groups that exists in real teaching learning situation. Permission was taken from the Dean, Faculty of Home Science and teachers teaching First Year. Periods (time) were secured in advance with the permission of the class teacher to conduct the film shows. Time plan was made and classes were fixed accordingly.

DATA COLLECTION

The data were collected in the month of March and April 1993 from First Year students of the Faculty of Home Science, M. S. University, Baroda.

For data collection, the groups formed by the Faculty office were used. There were six groups in all viz., A, B, C, D, E and F. Each group was further divided into three sub-groups viz. A1, A2, A3, B1, B2, B3, C1, C2, C3, D1, D2, D3, E1, E2, E3, F1, F2, and F3 for attending the practical classes. Each group was exposed to the seven video films separately. Care was taken to see that there were no clashes of classes among all the groups.

Before starting the experiment, the researcher with the help of class teacher of First year, administered the Questionnaire and collected data on personal factors, SES, modernity and personality of the respondents.

CONDUCTING THE EXPERIMENT

The experiment was carried out from March 1993 to April 1993. This experiment consisted of pre and post-test design. Therefore, the experiment involved three distinct stages:

(a) Pretest

(b) Experimental teaching

(c) Posttest

Administering the Pretest

The pretest was conducted with the group just before teaching through video film. The pretest had knowledge test items based on the content covered in the video film.

Experimental Teaching

Experimental teaching with the video film was done after conducting the pretest for all seven video films.

Administering the Posttest

The posttest was administered immediately after the video teaching.

The researcher personally with the help of two assistants took the classes of First Year for experimentation. One theory class of 55 minutes was taken for one session of pretest, experimental teaching and posttest. Thus, each group had seven classes of teaching of the selected units of "Women and Law" through seven video films.

SCORING AND CATEGORIZATION

For scoring and categorization of data, different procedures were used. The weightage was given to all the items of the questionnaire. The total number of respondents which might fall in each category was divided by the scores which they received. The scores of the respondents were considered for deciding the range of each category.

The first part of the questionnaire contained questions regarding background information of the respondents of the study. No scoring had to be done for this part and the variables were categorised directly according to the questions.

Variable	*Categories*	*Range of Score*
Stream in Higher Secondary	Arts	–
	Science	–
	Commerce	–
	Any other	–
Medium of instruction	English	–
	Gujarati	–
	Any other	–
Place of residence	City	
	Town	
	Village	–
Choosing Major	Related to Science	12
	Related to Social Science	
Legal education in family	LL.B. LL.M.	0-10-1
	Family's social work background	0-1
Involvement in Legal cases		0-1
Mother's occupation		0-1
Exposure to television and video		

Scores were given to the students for this variable, as shown. The possible scores ranged from least (0) to maximum (37). The respondents were divided into two categories under this variable as follows.

Criterion	*Range of Score*	*Category*
Below mean	0-18	Less exposure
Mean and above	19 and above	More exposure

Second part of the questionnaire had items to measure socio-economic status of the respondents. The scoring was done according to Desai Standardized scoring pattern, 1987. (Appendix–IV).

The categorization was done as follows:

Variables	*Category*	*Range of Score*
Socio-economic status	High	26-35
	Middle	21-25
	Low	0-20

Third part of the questionnaire had items to measure level of overall modernity. The scoring was done according to the Alex Inkele's scoring pattern, 1974 (Appendix–V). The categorization was done as follows:

Variable	*Category*	*Range of Score*
Overall	Modern	8-13
Modernity	Conservative	4 -17

The fourth part of the questionnaire had items to measure personality of the respondents. The scoring was done accordingly to A. Hafeez and V.S. Shanthamani scoring pattern/1974. (Appendix–VI). The categorization was done as follows:

Range of Score	*Personality traits*
8-10	High extroversion
5-10	High introversion
below 8 in extroversion } below 5 in introversion }	Ambiversion

For the variable Academic achievement, the office record was used by the researcher by obtaining the percentage of the marks secured by the First Year B. Sc. (Home) students in the Board examinations of twelfth standard. The categorisation was done as follows.

Variable	*Categories*	*Scores*
Academic achievement	High	60-75 1st division
	Low	45-59 IInd division

For the variable of competence in English, the student's previous semester's grade in English subject was taken as an indicator of their competence in English. The grades for the English course were collected from Faculty examination office. The respondents were divided into two categories according to the grades secured by them in English subject in first semester in the seven point scale. They were as follows:

English grade	*Category of competence*
B and above	Good
C and below	Poor

Knowledge Tests: As discussed before, the knowledge tests were completely objective in nature. Each correct answer was given a score of one and the incorrect answer was given zero score. The maximum obtainable score for one knowledge test was 20. A key was prepared for scoring the tests. Thus, seven tests were made to check the knowledge gain from seven video films.

ANALYSIS OF DATA

The data of the present investigation were analysed by employing the IBM PC/AT 386 compatible computer system.

Statistics used for analysis of data:

	Purpose	*Statistics*
1.	Distribution of the respondents in terms of personal and demographic characteristics	Percentages
2.	To study the gain in knowledge through the video films regarding "Women and Law". For overall and each category of all the variables for both pre-test and post test.	Mean Values
3.	To find out the significant differences in the mean scores of pre test and post test of the respondents.	*Paired 't[1] test*
4	Analysis of Covariance technique was applied to judge difference in effect due to variable. Analysis of Covariance represents an extension of analysis of variance to allow for the correlation between initial and final scores. Analysis of covariance is specially useful to the researcher when for various reasons it is impossible to equate groups on the criterion variable under study. Through covariance analysis, one is able to adjust the effect in terminal scores which will allow for differences in an initial stage.	*ANCOVA*

The method used for statistical analysis helped the investigator to meet the objectives and check the research hypothesis leading to conclusion based on the findings regarding effectiveness of the video films in imparting information regarding "Women and Law", and the selected variables.

CHAPTER 4

FINDINGS AND DISCUSSIONS

The present study was undertaken with the main purpose of developing a course on "Women and Law" for Home Science students, and developing video package to teach some parts of the course through video films to teach the first year students of Faculty of Home Science.

A quasi experiment was conducted to study the effectiveness of the video package in relation to the selected variables in teaching the course "Women and Law", to Home Science students.

The relevant data were obtained from 279 first year Home Science students in the year 1993 from the Faculty of Home Science, Baroda.

The frequency, percentage, mean scores, t-test, analysis of covariance were used to analyse the data.

This chapter deals with the findings of the study as follows:

1. Developing outline for the course "Women and Law".
2. Developing video package on "Women and Law".
3. Variablewise distribution of the respondents.
4. Overall effectiveness of the seven video films on "Women and Law".
5. Effectiveness of the seven video films in relation to the selected variables.
6. Conclusions and implications based on the findings.

DEVELOPING OUTLINE FOR THE COURSE "WOMEN AND LAW"

Content analysis of laws, related courses generated new understanding about planning the course "Women and Law", systematic scrutiny of the obtainable information indicated the neglected needs, on the basis of which conclusions for a suitable and feasible course outline for "Women and Law", were drawn as follows:

1. The achievable objectives of an introductory course "Women and Law" can be at the level of cognitive domain and aim at developing understanding of the laws. Such a course will be offered as a part of Home Science curriculum at undergraduate level.
2. Such a course would have only theory component wherever possible, discussion-with lawyers and trip to local court as well as some dramatization can be used for this course to make the course relevant and interesting.
3. For the organization of subject matter, the format containing objectives, main units, sub units and references were selected to enhance ease in following the subject matter. Related references are necessarily given as there is a wide variety of literature available on laws containing highly technical facts.

Thus, keeping the need and feasibility in mind following course outline was developed:

Course: Women and Law

Credit: 3

Level: Undergraduate.

Major Objective

To create awareness and understanding among the students regarding laws concerning women.

Specific Objectives

1. To make the students understand the importance of legal aspects in protecting women's rights.

2. To acquaint the students with different general laws concerning women and family welfare.
3. To develop awareness and understanding among the students regarding personal laws related to women.
4. To develop awareness and understanding among the students regarding women and social welfare legislation.

Contents

Unit I

1. Introduction
2. Women and the Constitution.
3. Directive Principles directly related to women.
4. Importance of protecting women's rights through legislature.

Unit II

Personal Laws

1. Hindu/Christian/ Parsi, Muslim in India in general.
2. Marriage-Valid, invalid, null and void.
3. Rights arising out of marriage.
4. Judicial separation, restitution of conjugal rights divorce, maintenance, criminal procedure of conjugal code.
5. Maintenance and custody of children.
6. Inheritance and Succession and transfer of property (movable and immovable) rights of spouse and children, joint and nuclear family rights/Hindu Succession Act, Indian Succession Act.

Unit III

Substantive Laws

1. Eve teasing (Section 352 of IPC)
2. Wife beating (Section 323 of IPC)
3. Cruelty on married women (Section 498 of IPC)
4. Rape (Section 375 of IPC)

Unit IV

Women and Social Welfare Legislation

1. Dowry Prohibition Act, 1961.
2. Medical Termination of Pregnancy Act, 1972.

References

1. Desai N., and Patel V., Indian women change and challenges in the International Decade 1975-85. Bombay, Popular Prakashan, 1985.
2. Sachidanand and Sinha, R.P., Women's rights: Myth and reality. Jaipur, Printwell Publishers, 1984.
3. Haksar, N., and Singh, A., Demystification of Law for Women. Lancer Press, New Delhi, 1986.
4. Government of India. Bare Acts. Government Press and Stationary Department, Baroda. 1970.
5. Mehta Rama. Divorced Hindu Women. Vikash Publication, Bombay, 1975.
6. Paul, M.C. Dowry and the position of women in India. Shakti Books, New Delhi, 1986.

DEVELOPING VIDEO PACKAGE ON "WOMEN AND LAW"

Seven video films making a compact package to teach undergraduate students were developed. The summary of the package is as follows:

Topic of the Unithg	*Title of the Film*	*Format*	*Type of the Film*
Introduction	Introduction to Law	Documentary, Interview.	Informative
Eve Teasing	Are you Eve Teased?	Documentary, Interview.	Informative
Inheritance	Law of Inheritance	Interview, Illustrative talk	Informative
Dowry	Is Dowry Legal?	Dramatization Illustrative talk	Persuasive Informative
Marriage	Marriage made easy with law	Dramatization Illustrative talk	Persuasive Informative
Divorce	Law of Divorce	Interview, Lecture	Informative
Rape	Trauma of Rape!	Lecture, Illustrative talk	Informative

Video films were developed in such a way that it achieves the objectives and yet presentation is done in an interesting and practical manner. The scripts of the video films were written keeping the selected content in mind. Since the films were made to impart information about various laws related to women, mainly the informative approach was used in writing the scripts.

All these films highlighted the personal laws related to women.

VARIABLEWISE DISTRIBUTION OF THE RESPONDENTS

The background information regarding the respondents' stream of study, medium of instruction, place of residence, social science inclination, legal background, social work background, mother's occupation, exposure to TV/video, socio economic status, modernity, personality, academic achievement, English competence, is presented in the Table 1.

Table 1

Variablewise Frequency and Percentage Distribution of First Year Home Science Students

N-279

Variable	*Category*	*Frequency*	*Percentage*
• **Stream**	Science	111	39.8
	General	168	60.2
• **Medium of Instruction**	English	156	55.9
	Any other	123	44.1
• **Place of Residence**	City	252	90.3
	Town/Village	27	9.7
• **Social Science Inclination**	Yes	164	58.8
	No	115	41.2
• **Legal Exposure**	Yes	76	27.2
	No	203	72.8
• **Social Work Background**	Yes	72	25.8
	No	207	74.2
• **Mother's Occupation**	Housewife	234	83.9
	Employed	45	16.1
• **Exposure to T.V./Video**	High	140	50.2
	Low	139	49.8
• **SES**	High	195	69.9
	Middle	73	26.2
	Low	11	3.9

Contd...

N-279

Variable	*Category*	*Frequency*	*Percentage*
• Modernity	Modern	225	80.6
	Conservative	54	19.4
• Personality	Introvert	44	15.8
	Ambivert	101	36.2
	Extrovert	134	48.0
• Academic Achievement	Low	154	55.2
	High	125	44.8
• English Competence	Low	119	42.7
	High	160	57.3

Sixty per cent of the students were from science stream as compared to nearly 40 % of the students who were from general stream as had studied in their higher secondary. The percentage of respondents who had offered general stream at school differed significantly in number. (Figure 1).

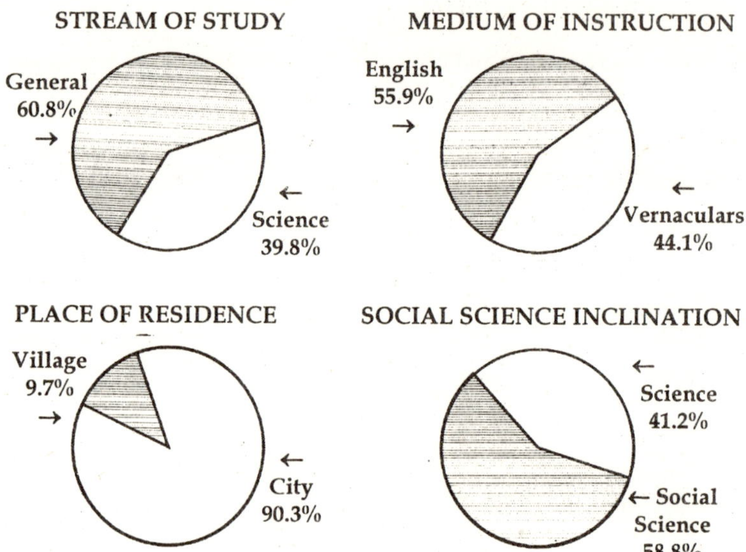

FIGURE 1

Fifty five per cent of the respondents had English as medium, of instruction at school, followed by 44 % who had studied through vernacular language, that is either Gujarati, Marathi or Hindi. (Figure 1).

An overwhelming majority of 90 % of the respondents were from urban area, and only 10% were found to be from town/ village. That means, Faculty of Home Science, Baroda has an overwhelming majority of urban students. (Figure 1).

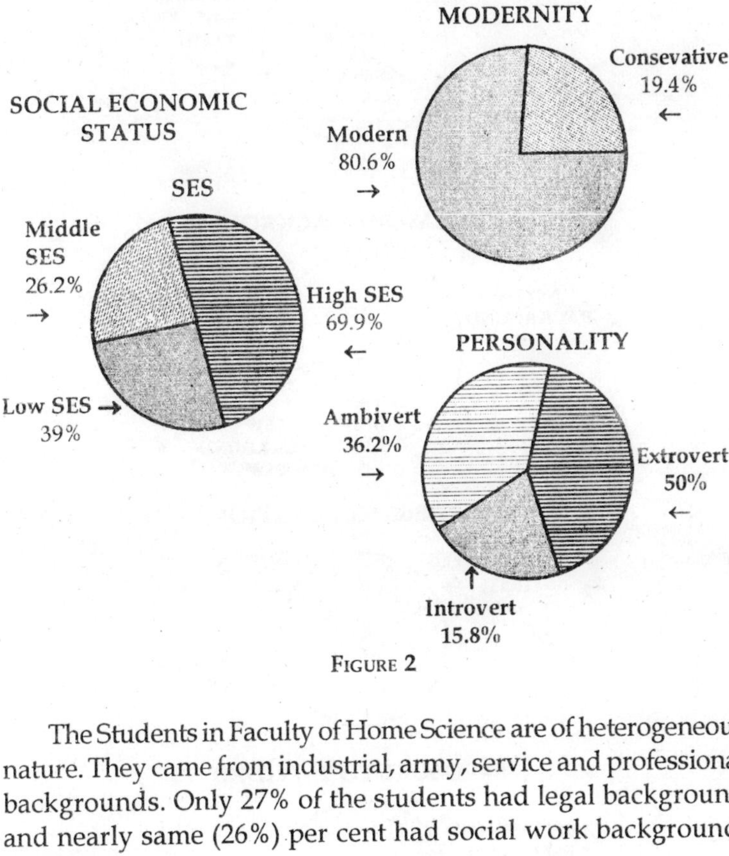

FIGURE 2

The Students in Faculty of Home Science are of heterogeneous nature. They came from industrial, army, service and professional backgrounds. Only 27% of the students had legal background and nearly same (26%) per cent had social work background. (Figure 3).

The data related to the mother's occupation showed that majority of the respondent's mothers were housewives, only 16 % of the respondents' mothers were engaged as employed women. It may be because majority of the students were from high and upper middle income group and they may not feel the need for employment in order to support the family financially. (Figure 3).

Respondents having high and low exposure to T.V. and video were almost equal in percentage. (Figure 3).

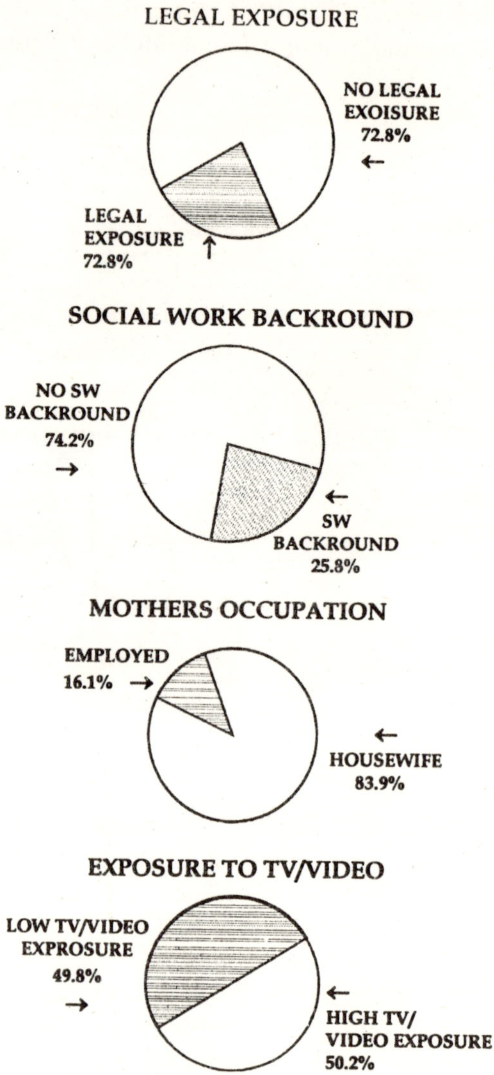

FIGURE 3

As seen in Table 1 majority of the respondents belonged to 'modern' category.

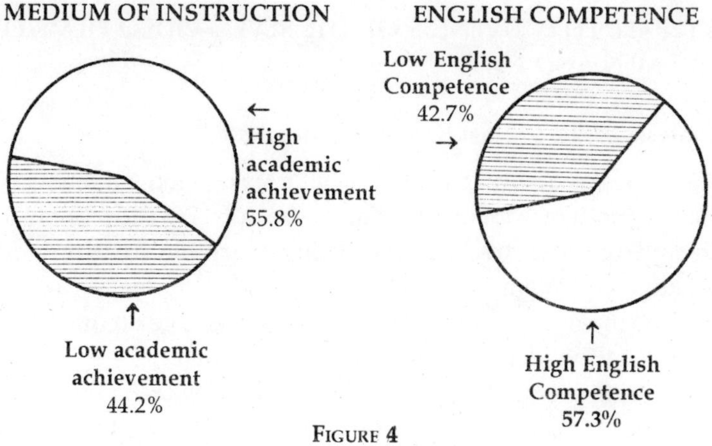

FIGURE 4

Only 16% of the Home Science students belonged to introvert personality, whereas, nearly 50% of the respondents were extroverts. That is, students had either ambivert or introvert. The ambivert gives evidence of behaviour that may be extravert in some situations and extrovert in others. For example, a person may be friendly but likes to work alone. Most of the people belong to the ambivert group. The Home Science students also showed this normal trend. More than 50% of the respondents had obtained second class in 12th standard, which was considered, low academic achievement in the present study. Whereas, only 44% of the respondents had obtained first class in 12th standard and had high academic achievement.

To conclude, it was found that first year students in majority were from general stream having urban background with high social science inclination and majority did not possess legal and social work background.

It was interesting to note that majority of the respondents were modern although their mothers were housewives. Nearly equal percentages of respondents were having high as well as low exposure to T.V. and video, and nearly 60% had high English competence, but low academic achievement. (Figure 4).

OVERALL EFFECTIVENESS OF THE SEVEN VIDEO FILMS ON "WOMEN AND LAW"

Analysis of the Pretest Scores of Knowledge

The pretest scores of the experiment revealed that on the whole the respondents obtained mean scores of 11 out of 20 on the knowledge test, irrespective of any variable for the video package on "Women and Law".

The mean scores of respondents' knowledge on the pretest according to video films is shown in Figure 5.

The respondents scored highest mean scores (13-49) for-the film on "Inheritance", and lowest (11.04) for the film on "Divorce".

The mean scores of the respondents for the "Introduction" film was almost same as those for the film on "Marriage".

On the whole, it was observed that the respondents scored low on the pretest of the knowledge test. The majority of respondents did not have adequate previous knowledge to respond to the knowledge test. The items on knowledge test were objective and required precision on part of the respondents. Therefore, even if they possessed general knowledge in the field of "Women and Law", they may not be able to apply it with precision as demanded.

Analysis of the Post Test Scores of Knowledge

On the whole, the mean score of the respondents on post test of the knowledge was 17 out of 20-which was considerably higher compared to their pretest mean scores which was only 11.

The mean scores of respondents on the post test of knowledge according to the video films is shown in Figure 6. The respondents scored highest for the film on Marriage 17.54 and lowest for the Introduction film 14.84. Further, the respondents scored almost equal for the film on "Eve Teasing" and "Divorce" as their mean scores were 16.04 and 16.70 respectively as revealed in Table 2.

MEAN SCORES OF KNOWLEDGE ON PRE-TEST AND POST-TEST OF THE RESPONDENTS ACCORDING TO THE VIDEO FILMS

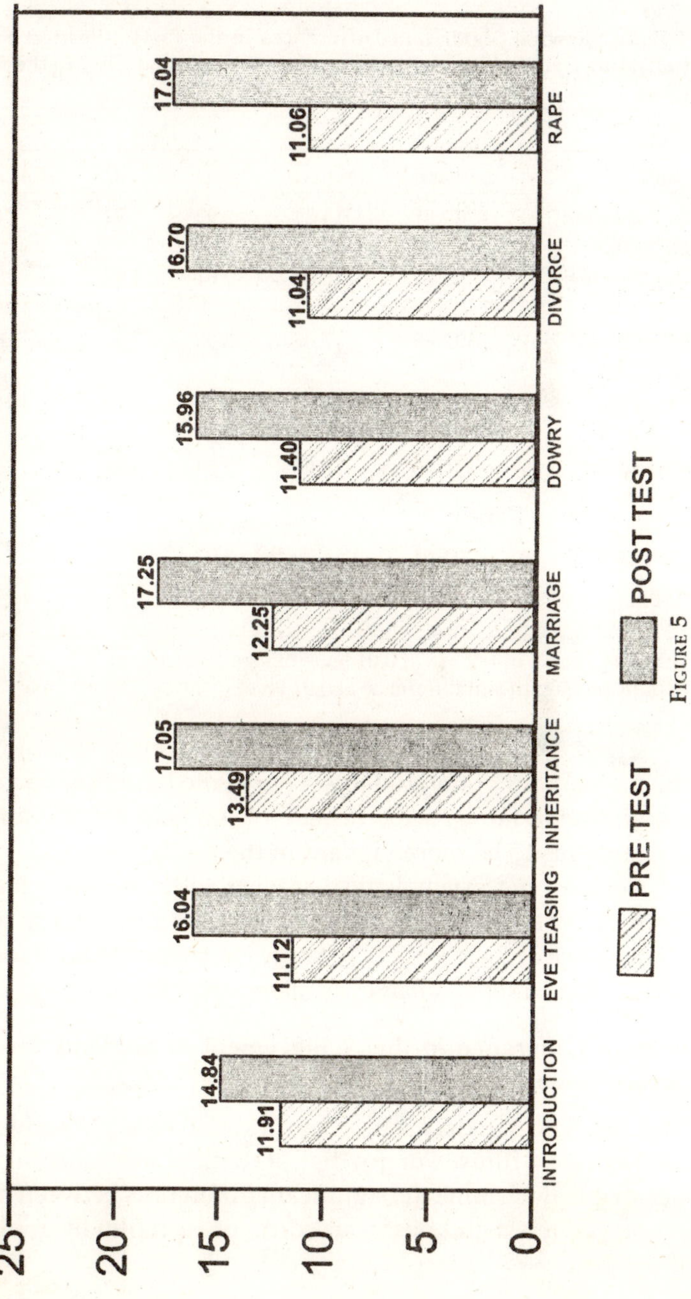

FIGURE 5

Table 2
T-Ratio Showing Significant Differences in the Pretest-Posttest Scores Indicating Gain in Knowledge Regarding "Women and Law" in the Seven Films

Topic	*X, Pretest*	*Posttest*	*S.D*	*D*	*t Value Calculated*
Introduction (N = 207)	11.91	14.84	2.92	2.92	14.42**
Eve Teasing (N = 225)	11.12	16.04	2.61	4.92	28.30**
Inheritance (N = 184)	13.49	17.05	2.55	3.55	18.89**
Marriage (N = 217)	12.25	17.54	3.12	5.29	24.95**
Dowry (N = 237)	11.40	15.96	2.63	4.56	26.70**
Divorce (N = 233)	11.04	16.70	2.97	5.65	29.03**
Rape (N = 215)	11.06	17.04	2.61	5.98	33.56**

Tabulated value of t=2.345 at 0.01 level of significance.
** Indicates significant difference at 0.01 level.

There could also be some personal reasons contributing to the motivations of the students. Those who have ever had such experience in family which needed legal help may be forcing the students to be more vigilant in the matter.

Besides, the psychological reasons to know laws, that is, the need for self protection, the students are aware of the social significance of the necessity to know the laws in today's society where crime rate is on an ever increasing rate.

Overall Difference in the Achievement of Students through Seven Video Films

The differences in the mean scores (Table 2) reflect effectiveness of the video films. For further statistical inference, it was decided to determine the significant differences between mean scores of pretest and post test scores for each film by applying the 't' test.

The spread of scores for the films as indicated by the magnitude of standard deviation was more or less same.

The respondents showed a significant difference in the mean scores of pretest and post test as indicated by the t-value of the seven films on "Women and Law". The t-value was found to be highly significant for all the seven video films on "Women and Law" indicating effectiveness of the video films. The scores of the respondents of the study revealed that on the whole, they showed significant gain from all the seven video films.

The Video film on "Rape" was most effective as t-value (33.56) indicates and the least effective film was on "Introduction to Law" with t-value (14.42). The film on "Rape" may have directed the respondents to think about themselves and moreover social pressure may have induced the students of the first year to give serious thought to their protection. Therefore, they are better oriented towards this law in comparison to others.

Table 2 further reveals that the respondents have obtained less scores for the film on Inheritance in comparison to other films. It is likely that the first year students have not given serious thought to this aspect as they are very young. The matter of Inheritance is very remote in their thinking and that is why they have scored less. Film on Eve-teasing, Marriage, Dowry and Divorce were almost equally effective and therefore, differences of t-value may not be very perceptible between these films.

The gain in knowledge as shown by the respondents, is a very encouraging feature, as it throws light on the effectiveness of films as well as on the acceptance of the course "Women and Law" by Home Science students.

Implication of the Findings Related to the Knowledge Gain

On the whole, the seven video films were effective. As discussed earlier video films were developed by taking great care and working out the minutest details of the content. Keeping in mind the suitability for the selected content the video films were made. Here, implication can be that for video teaching a teacher should thoroughly check the appropriateness of the content.

Besides this reason, the students of Home Science must have found video teaching as a novel experience as it is not very common for them to learn through video.

The content on "Women and Law" was such that it gives association of ideas, more familiarity and application of knowledge as a starting point. All these characteristics were likely to contribute to better learning. Consideration of familiarity with topic as a starting point, might have resulted into more meaningful learning which might have aroused curiosity and eagerness to learn. Moreover, to make the films effective each law was explained as far as possible with visual aids. Each film was summarised with major points at the end to help students recapitulate the law. This might have helped them to perform equally well throughout in all the seven films. Therefore, it can be implied that while teaching through video films good organization of content should be followed throughout.

The teachers teaching the course "Women and Law" could make an effort to emphasize main laws involved in the content. To promote active understanding of the subject "Women and Law" in Home Science, it would be advisable to teach "Women and Law" as an integrative thread for the undergraduate level.

It is impossible that exposure to subject matter alone will result into productive learning. Therefore, it need to be carefully designed and directed objectives of the course "Women and Law". Learning experiences should be comprehensive to cover the entire subject matter. They should develop understanding and ability to relate and apply the knowledge.

Each learning experience should arouse sufficient curiosity. This can be achieved if teachers continuously stress the relationships and provide broad meaningful context in which the students acquire knowledge.

Besides the above academic reason there could be another reason for the respondents to show keenness to learn because the crime rate against women is increasing and T.V., radio and other mass media are trying to educate people. All this is given too much importance and publicity by the various women's voluntary and governmental organizations. As a result, women today are looking for their future in a broader perspective, than before. They are realising the importance of knowing laws in their lives which is now considered important for safety/ security and self defence.

Besides this, feminist groups are organising different seminars, street plays and workshops. This might have helped the students in their increased interest in learning the course. Certain social reasons could be contributing to learn "Women and Law". Baroda being a cosmopolitan city, girls get wider exposure to the different types of experiences. It also affects the attitudes towards knowing legal procedures. It is needed in everyday routine life.

EFFECTIVENESS OF VIDEO FILMS IN RELATION TO THE SELECTED VARIABLES

In this section the findings regarding the effectiveness of video films in relation to the Stream of Study, Medium of Instruction, Place of Residence, Social Science Inclination, Legal Exposure, Social Work Background, Mother's Occupation, TV/Video Exposure, Socio Economic Status, Modernity, Personality, Academic Achievement and English Competence are reported as follows.

To find out the difference in gain in knowledge because of the variables in relation to the video films, preliminary analysis was done by using the test of ANCOVA. The test of ANCOVA revealed in general, differences in learning due to the variables. The variations in learning due to the variables in general are represented in the form of calculated F-values in the ANCOVA tables.

The data were further analysed by using paired t-test to find out the exact significant differences among the respondents due to the variables. The t-values represent the differences in the pre-post scores for each variables.

Thus, all the 13 variables were first analysed in general by sing ANCOVA tests. Further analysis was carried out by using paired t-tests to find out the specific differences in the gain in knowledge due to videos regarding "Women and Law".

Stream of Study

In this section the findings regarding the effectiveness of video films in relation to the stream of study is presented. The preliminary analysis was done to find out the differences in learning because of the stream of study. This analysis results are presented in the ANCOVA Table 3. This ANCOVA table 3 presents the general variation in learning due to the variable stream of study.

Table 3

ANCOVA, Showing Significance of Differences in the Post Scores after Removing the Effect of Pre Scores in the Knowledge by Learning Through the Video Films on "Women and Law", and the Stream of Study

Source of Variation-Films		*SS*	*DF*	*MSS*	*F Value*
Introduction	Treatment	1359.05	2-1=1	22.50	4.76*
	Within	964.12	206-2=204	4.72	
	Total	22.50	206		
Eve Teasing	Treatment	16.94	2-1=1	16.94	5.27*
	Within	713.48	224-2=222	3.21	
	Total	762.46	224		
Inheritance	Treatment	42.93	2-1=1	42.93	14.41**
	Within	539.20	183-2=181	2.97	
	Total	667.45	183		
Marriage	Treatment	13.20	2-1=1216	13.20	3.56
	Within	792.50	216-2=214	3.70	
	Total	835.83			
Dowry	Treatment	29.15	2-1=1	29.15	9.61**
	Within	709.63	236-2=234	3.03	
	Total	778.65	236		
Divorce	Treatment	106.86	2-1=1	106.86	23.82**
	Within	1031.46	232-2=230	4.48	
	Total	1262.56	232		
Rape	Treatment	90.08	2-1=1	90.08	23.42**
	Within	815.36	214-2=212	3.84	
	Total	1135.53	214		

Indicates significant difference at 0.05 level.
** Indicates significant difference at 0.01 level.
Tab. F-Value at 0.05 = 3.89 and at 0.01 = 6.76

Maximum differences in gain of knowledge were found for the films on Rape/Divorce and Inheritance according to stream of study. The knowledge gained by Science and general stream students differed significantly as indicated by F-values in Table 3.

However, the effect of stream of study was found to be minimum for the film on Marriage. That is, the content on Marriage was learnt equally well by the Science and general stream students as F-value is found to be insignificant in Table 3.

The null hypothesis stated that there will be no significant difference in knowledge gain in terms of pre-post scores of the students according to the stream of study at higher secondary school level. However, analysis of overall knowledge gain in relation to the stream of study showed highly significant differences. So, the null hypothesis was partially accepted. That is, accepted in case of film on marriage and not accepted for rest of the six films.

The Table 4 further presents the pre-post scores of each film with reference to Stream of Study. It is apparent that according to Table 4 the pretest scores for all the seven video films were almost equal for the students from Science as well as general streams. That is, to begin with both the

Table 4

Distribution of the T-Ratio, Showing Significant Difference in Pretest-Posttest Scores of Respondents on the Seven Video Films in Relation to Stream of Study

Video Films	*Stream of Study*	X_1 *Pretest*	X_2 *Posttest*	*Cal.t Value*	*Tab .t .01*
Introduction	Science N = 79	13.03	15.70	9.78**	2.37
	General N = 128	11.22	14.31	10.95**	2.35
Eve Teasing	Science N = 87	11.24	16.41	22.19**	2.37
	General N = 138	11.05	15.81	19.67**	2.35
Inheritance	Science N = 93	13.84	17.62	14.39**	2.36
	General N = 91	13.13	16.47	12.36**	2.36
Marriage	Science N =100	12.10	17.79	21.63**	2.36
	General N = 117	12.38	17.33	15.45**	2.35
Dowry	Science N = 90	11.10	16.35	18.35**	2.35
	General N = 147	11.58	15.72	20.14**	2.35
Divorce	Science N = 88	11.11	17.59	22.80**	2.37
	General N =145	11.00	16.16	20.37**	2.35
Rape	Science N = 92	11.17	17.83	25.00**	2.36
	General N = 123	10.98	16.45	23.81**	2.35

**Indicates significant difference at 0.01 level.

streams of students possessed nearly equal knowledge as indicated by the pretest scores. However, the posttest scores indicate higher gain in knowledge by the Science stream students. In all the seven video films, Science stream students have gained higher mean scores in comparison to general stream students.

Differences between the pretest-posttest scores were found to be highly significant as indicated by t-value in Table 4. Irrespective of the stream of study, the students found the video films to be interesting and effective as indicated by significant high posttest scores.

It was also noticed that the Science stream respondents gained considerably higher than the general stream respondents. It can be because the Science students may have developed an ability to think more logically due to their background.

This would imply that the Faculty can continue the practice of grouping the First Year Home Science students. That is, all the Science group students together and general stream students together. This provides more homogeneity in their background and results into more effective and productive learning.

It will also help in deciding learning experiences and content. Due to a homogeneous previous background in the stream of study, the students may have similar capacity to grasp the knowledge, it will help the teachers to decide the suitable pace of learning also. Moreover* there would be convenience in teaching and accelerated learning would result due to streamwise grouping.

To conclude it can be said that we should admit more Science students in Faculty of Home Science, at the same time should not avoid general stream students as they have also learnt the content on "Women and Law".

Medium of Instruction

Again Table 5, is based on ANCOVA and it will show generally speaking the differences between learning of laws and the medium of instruction at school level.

Table 5
ANCOVA, Showing Significance of Differences in the Post Scores After Removing the Effect of Pre Scores in the Knowledge by Learning Through the Video Films on "Women and Law" and the Medium of Instruction

Source of Variation-Films		*SS*	*DF*	*MSS*	*F Value*
Introduction	Treatment	65.45	2-1=1	20664.45	14.25**
	Within	922.17	206-2=204	4.52	
	Total	1359.05	206		
Eve Teasing	Treatment	99.00	2-1=1	99.00	34.80**
	Within	631.43	224-2=222	2.84	
	Total	762.46	224		
Inheritance	Treatment	109.03	2-1=1	109.03	41.71**
	Within	473.09	183-2=181	2.61	
	Total	667.45	183		
Marriage	Treatment	84.11	2-1=1	84.11	24.94**
	Within	721.59	216-2=214	3.37	
	Total	835.83	216		
Dowry	Treatment	64.34	2-1=1	64.34	22.32**
	Within	674.44	236-2=234	2.88	
	Total	778.65	236		
Divorce	Treatment	202.21	2-1=1	202.21	49.68**
	Within	936.10	232-2=230	4.07	
	Total	1262.56	232		
Rape	Treatment	102.37	2-1=1	102.37	27.02**
	Within	803.07	214-2=212	3.78	
	Total	1135.53	214		

"Indicates significant difference at 0.01 level.
Tab. F-Value at 0.05 = 3.89 and at 0.01 = 6.76

It was found that the observed values of F for Medium of Instruction was highly significant. This shows that the students from English medium did differ significantly from the students from other medium, Maximum difference was found for the film on Divorce (49.68) and film on Inheritance (41.71). The reason for this big difference could be that in these two films more of lecture method was used, where laws were taught by lawyers by lecture method which were mainly in English. The students from other medium of instruction must have found it difficult to grasp the content which was mainly in English. So, they could not do as well as the English medium students did in the post test. Handal (1991) also found that the respondents having poor English background faced more academic problems, as compared to the respondents with good English background.

Hence, the null hypothesis stating that there will be no significant difference in the knowledge gain in terms of pre- % post scores of the students according to the medium of instruction at school level was not accepted as the effect of the medium of instruction was found to be highly significant in Table 5.

Table 6 shows that analysis of t-distribution. To find out difference in the pre-post test scores due to variable Medium of Instruction t-test was computed.

Table 6

Distribution of the T-Ratio, Showing Significant Differences in Pretest-Posttest Scores of the Respondents on the Seven Video Films in Relation to Medium of Instruction

Video Films	*Medium of Instruction at School*	X_1 *Pre-test*	X_2 *Post-test*	*Cal t Value*	*Tab. t Value 0.01*
Introduction	English Medium N = 116	12.95	15.73	11.17**	2.364
	Other Medium N = 97	10.59	13.71	9.27**	2.368
Eve Teasing	English Medium N = 128	11.26	16.64	26.08**	2.358
	Other Medium N = 91	10.93	15.25	15.01**	2.368
Inheritance	English Medium N = 110	13.61	17.71	16.99**	2.364
	Other Medium N = 74	13.31	16.06	9.91**	2.381
Marriage	English Medium N = 129	12.55	18.09	21.21**	2.358
	Other Medium N = 88	11.81	16.73	13.91**	2.374
Dowry	English Medium N = 137	11.49	16.42	22.97**	2.358
	Other Medium N = 100	11.27	15.33	14.93**	2.364
Divorce	English Medium N = 130	11.45	17.63	25.70**	2.358
	Other Medium N = 103	10.53	15.53	16.17**	2.364
Rape	English Medium N = 122	11.36	17.76	30.12**	2.358
	Other Medium N = 93	10.66	16.10	18.39**	2.368

*Indicates Significant difference at 0.01 level.

Table 6, shows that there were more students from English medium in comparison to other medium. Further analysis of table shows that the mean scores of pretest revealed that the students with English background achieved higher compared to the students from vernacular medium as shown in Table 6. The analysis of the post test scores also showed the similar trend. The respondents from English medium gained higher in comparison to the students from other medium. Overall difference in the achievement of students according to the medium of instruction was found to be highly significant as indicated by value of t. The video films were found to be effective as students learnt the content on "Women and Law", irrespective of their English medium background. However, the respondents from English background gained significantly higher knowledge. The reason for this could be that the video films were in English, which must have facilitated the understanding of the students of English medium.

Moreover, keeping in view the national development as the objective the Education Commission (12964-66) comments:

> Even after the regional language became the media of higher education in the university, a working knowledge of English will be available asset for all students, and, a reasonable proficiency in English language will be necessary for those who proceed to the university.

Many of the colleges and universities have English as the medium of instruction. The students coming from vernacular medium schools face many problems related to English when they join college. Arora (1977) investigated that in the area of language the low achievers of all the three classes, that is, 1st, 2nd and 3rd year students of Faculty of Home Science reported that, sometimes they could not express well in the class, had difficulty in asking and answering questions in the class and could not express while writing test and assignments. A higher percentage of the respondents having poor background of English were facing more problems regarding language as compared to the respondents having good medium of English.

To conclude, it can be said that since the medium of instruction of M.S. University is English and English continues to be the medium of instruction at the Faculty of Home Science, Baroda, the admission criteria of passing school examination with English as a subject may not suffice but they should also include the medium of English as one of the criteria. Since, English was the medium of instruction for video teaching, it might be possible that the respondents who came from English medium could understand the instructions better as compared to those who came from vernacular schools. Thus, respondents with English medium scored higher than the respondents with other medium.

Place of Residence

This section comprises of findings of the effectiveness of video films in relation to the place of residence. In this era of modernization the village unit is undergoing a gradual transformation. Technological advancement in the country has brought about changes in the family. Greater geographical and occupational mobility have gradually changed the traditional conceptions regarding the place and role of women in contemporary Indian Society. The urban and educated people are already beginning to realise the importance of knowing laws, but it is the huge rural population which has yet to develop such legal awareness. There is a growing recognition about cultural factors having an important bearing on any development process. The investigator wanted to find out the effect of the place of residence and the gain in knowledge regarding "Women and Law", when taught through video.

ANCOVA was computed to determine effect of the place of residence on the knowledge gain. The F-value indicates such an effect in Table 7. Further probe into the findings revealed that respondents from city as well village were equally benefited through video films on "Women and Law". When the hypothesis that there will be no significant difference in knowledge gain in terms of pre-post scores of the students according to place of residence was tested, the data revealed that the calculated F-values were not significant for six video films on "Women and Law". However, for the film on 'Eve teasing[1] the F-value was found significant at 0.05 level of confidence as in Table 7. So, the null hypothesis was partially accepted, that is, accepted in case of the six video films, while not accepted in case of the film on 'Eve teasing'.

Table 7

ANCOVA, Showing Significance of Differences in the Post Scores After Removing the Effect of Pre Scores in the Knowledge by Learning Through the Video Films on "Women and Law" and the Place of Residence

Source of Variation-Films		*SS*	*DF*	*MSS*	*F Value*
Introduction	Treatment	15.84	2-1=1	15.84	3.33
	Within	970.78	206-2=204	4.75	
	Total	1359.05	206		
Eve Teasing	Treatment	14.91	2-1=1	14.91	4.62*
	Within	715.52	224-2=222	3.22	
	Total	762.46	224		
Inheritance	Treatment	6.06	2-1=1	6.06	1.90
	Within	576.06	183-2=181	3.18	
	Total	667.45	183		
Marriage	Treatment	8.84	2-1=1	8.84	2.37
	Within	796.86	216-2=214	3.72	
	Total	835.83	216		
Dowry	Treatment	1.04	2-1=1	1.04	0.33
	Within	737.74	236-2=234	3.15	
	Total	778.65	236		
Divorce	Treatment	0.67	2-1=1	0.67	0.13
	Within	1137.65	232-2=230	4.94	
	Total	1262.56	232		
Rape	Treatment	15.34	2-1=1	15.34	3.65
	Within	890.10	214-2=212	4.19	
	Total	1135.53	214		

* Indicates significant difference at 0.05 level,
Tab. F-Value at 0.05 = 3.89

In other words, variable 'Place of Residence' did not make much impact on learning of laws related to women. The probable reason for this could be as explained by Arora (1977) who commented that the influences of urbanization and industrialization has brought about a greater degree of non-traditionalism in the outlook of our village people.

Conditions of rural India have changed a great deal with the starting of community projects, agricultural extension services, industries and the increased communication facilities. The fast changing social and cultural environment may have an effect on the way of life of the village people.

According to Table 8 there was low mean scores in pretest. However, after video teaching it increased as evident from high post test scores for all the seven video films.

Table 8

Distribution of the T-Ratio Showing Significant Differences in Pretest-Posttest Scores of Respondents on the Seven Video Films in Relation to Place of Residence

Video Films	*Place of Residence*	X_1 *Pre-test*	X_2 *Post-test*	*Cal t Value*	*Tab. t Value 0.01*
Introduction	City N = 191	11.97	14.79	13.56**	2.345
	Town/Village N =16	11.18	15.50	5.23**	2.584
Eve Teasing	City N ≐ 200	11.12	16.14	27.57**	2.345
	Town/Village N = 25	11.12	15.32	7.39**	2.345
Inheritance	City N = 170	13.52	17.01	17.67**	2.352
	Town/Village N = 14	13.07	17.57	7.50**	2.624
Marriage	City N = 195	12.20	17.60	24.13**	2.345
	Town/Village N = 22	12.68	17.00	6.76**	2.508
Dowry	City N = 216	11.39	15.98	26.46**	2.345
	Town/Village N = 21	11.47	15.76	5.74**	2.518
Divorce	City N = 210	11.09	16.09	28.02**	2.345
	Town/Village N = 23	10.65	16.43	7.89**	2.500
Rape	City N = 196	11.11	17.14	33.08**	2.345
	Town/Village N = 19	10.57	16.00	7.42 **	2.540

* Indicates significant difference at 0.01 level.

The findings of Table 8, revealed that larger per cent of the respondents came from city. It was assumed that the learning of laws may be affected by the place of residence because a student from city may have new ideas and new ways of thinking and acting, compared to a student from village. In India, 80 % of population resides in 568,000 villages, so it may affect the quality of life. Table 8, shows that students from urban area learnt more about laws regarding eve teasing in comparison to rural area. The probable reason for this could be that the incidence of eve teasing is more common in cities. So these girls from the city are finding the need to be more aware of laws related to eve-teasing, so that they can take necessary action to protect themselves.

Findings of Tables 7 and 8, can be concluded that each video film when shown to the two categories of students was found to be effective. The rural as well as urban the students both could very well learn the content on "Women and Law". As small number of rural students are there and yet they have learnt significantly, rural students should be encouraged and we should not discriminate against students on the basis of their place of residence. On the whole, students from city as well as village learnt significantly through all the video films.

Social Science Inclination

As already discussed in the Chapter 3 of Methodology, the students were asked to indicate their inclination towards Social Sciences. Thus, in the present investigation, the students were categorized into two groups, one with social science inclination and the other having science inclination.

The null hypothesis was that there will be no significant difference in knowledge gain in terms of pre-post scores of the students according to the inclination towards social science.

Significant differences were found in the pre-post scores of the students according to the inclination towards social science. As shown in Table 9, the F-value was highly significant for the 6 video films and was insignificant for one video film. So, the null hypothesis was partially not accepted, that is, accepted in case of film on marriage and not accepted for the rest of the six video films on "Women and Law".

Table 9

ANCOVA, Showing Significance of Differences in the Post Scores After Removing the Effect of Pre Scores in the, Knowledge by Learning Through the Video Films on "Women and Law", and the Social Science Inclination

Source of Variation-Films		*SS*	*DF*	*MSS*	*F Value*
Introduction	Treatment	21.03	2-1=1	21.03	4.44*
	Within	965.59	206-2=204	4.73	
	Total	1359.05	206		
Eve Teasing	Treatment	55.90	2-1=1	55.90	18.39**
	Within	674.53	224-2=222	3.03	
	Total	762.46	224		
Inheritance	Treatment	37.45	2-1=1	37.45	12.44**
	Within	544.68	183-2=181	3.00	
	Total	667.45	183		
Marriage	Treatment	8.22	2-1=1	8.22	2.20
	Within	797.48	216-2=214	3.72	
	Total	835.83	216		
Dowry	Treatment	44.46	2-1=1	44.46	14.98**
	Within	694.33	236-2=234	2.96	
	Total	778.65	236		
Divorce	Treatment	68.77	2-1=1	68.77	14.78**
	Within	1069.55	232-2=230	4.65	
	Total	1262.56	232		
Rape	Treatment	74.83	2-1=1	74.83	19.09**
	Within	830.61	214-2=212	3.91	
	Total	1135.53	214		

*Indicates significant difference at 0.05 level.
** Indicates significant difference at 0.01 level.
Tab. F-Value at 0.05 = 3.89 and at 0.01 = 6.76

Out of all the seven video films the film, on Marriage was learnt equally well by both the groups as evident from insignificant F-value (Table 9). The laws for Marriage ware learnt by both the groups through the video film the reason for this is^ that the video film, on Marriage was having part of it in Gujarati and main points were repeated in English. So, both the groups found it interesting and equally effective. This implies that Law is teachable to both the types of students whether with science inclination or social science inclination.

We should teach Personal Laws to students from social science inclination as well as to the students with science inclination.

As evident from Table 10, the pretest scores of both the groups of students having social science inclination as well as having science inclination scored nearly equal marks. The t-value gives the exact differences'in the pre-post scores.

Table 10

Distribution of the T-Ratio, Showing Significant Differences in Pretest-Posttest Scores of Respondents on the Seven Video Films in Relation to Social Science Inclination

Video Films	*Social Science Inclination*	X_1 *Pre-test*	X_2 *Post-test*	*Cal t Value*	*Tab. t Value 0.01*
Introduction	Social Science N = 126	11.43	14.39	10.35**	2.358
	Science Inclination N = 81	12.66	15.54	10.69**	2.374
Eve Teasing	Social Science N = 132	11.15	15.63	19.05**	2.358
	Science Inclination N = 93	11.07	16.63	22.84**	2.368
Inheritance	Social Science N = 98	13.26	16.26	12.88**	2.368
	Science Inclination N = 86	13.75	17.60	13.97**	2.374
Marriage	Social Science N = 122	12.22	17.36	17.74**	2.358
	Science Inclination N = 95	12.28	17.76	17.65**	2.368
Dowry	Social Science N = 143	11.42	15.61	19.90**	2.358
	Science Inclination N = 94	11.36	16.48	18.38**	2.368
Divorce	Social Science N = 141	11.06	16.26	19.32**	2.358
	Science Inclination N = 92	11.02	17.36	24.84**	2.368
Rape	Social Science N = 127	11.09	16.56	23.34**	2.358
	Science Inclination N = 88	11.02	17.73	26.23**	2.374

** Indicates significant difference at 0.01 level.

However, after the video teaching, the students having science inclination gained more knowledge as indicated by their higher posttest mean scores in all the seven video films on "Women and Law". As shown in Table 10, the calculated t-value for pretest-posttest of all the seven video films for both the groups, with social science inclination and with science inclination were found to be highly significant at 0.01 level of confidence. This means that the students' achievement differed significantly in the two tests.

Further analysis of t-value indicates that films on Rape (19.09), Eve-teasing (18.39), were most effective for the students with science inclination. It seems, it was not the content which was more attractive for the students with science inclination but the English language. The reason for these findings could be that as the content of these films were in English, so it was easy for them to learn and understand it. Mandal (1991) found that students performing at the lowest level in the college had significantly poor background in English. The English background was significantly higher for the high achievers in the college.

One further thought is, that whether they opted for science or social science inclination they are young women and therefore–their perception of need for Personal Laws could be the same. The findings strengthen the researcher's view that personal laws should be taught to all the women students regardless of their inclination towards social science or just science.

It can be concluded, that each video film for the two categories of students was found to be effective. Overall, both with and without social science inclination respondents learnt significantly through video films on "Women and Law".

Legal Exposure

The effectiveness of video films in relation to the Legal Exposure is presented in this section.

It was assumed that legal exposure of the family members would exert some kind of impression on the knowledge gain regarding "Women and Law". A legal exposure generally meant that either parents or family members had legal profession or they were involved in some legal procedures.

Findings of feasibility study showed that there were different sources of information regarding law for the First Year students of Faculty of Home Science. The sources were grouped as formal and informal. Among the informal sources, family was found to be the most popular source of information about the law, followed by friends and neighbours.

Further probe into Table 11 shows that the students with or without legal exposure benefitted more or less equally through video films on "Women and Law". But significant difference in gain existed for 4 films. The F-values for these 4 films namely, Introduction (6.03), Eve-teasing (5.80) Rape (3.91)

Table 11

ANCOVA, Showing Significance of Differences in the Post Scores After Removing the Effect of Pre Scores in the Knowledge by Learning Through the Video Films on "Women and Law" and the Legal Exposure of Family

Source of Variation-Films		*SS*	*DF*	*MSS*	*F Value*
Introduction	Treatment	28.35	2-1=1	28.35	6.03*
	Within	958.27	206-2=204	4.69	
	Total	1359.05	206		
Eve Teasing	Treatment	18.62	2-1=1	18.62	5.80*
	Within	711.80	224-2=222	3.20	
	Total	762.46	224		
Inheritance	Treatment	0.47	2-1=1	0.47	0.14
	Within	581.66	183-2=181	3.21	
	Total	667.45	183		
Marriage	Treatment	24.78	2-1=1	24.78	6.79**
	Within	780.92	216-2=214	3.64	
	Total	835.83	216		
Dowry	Treatment	9.44	2-1=1	9.44	3.03
	Within	729.34	236-2=234	3.11	
	Total	778.65	236		
Divorce	Treatment	0.34	2-1=1	0.34	0.07
	Within	1137.97	232-2=230	4.94	
	Total	1262.56	232		
Rape	Treatment	16.41	2-1=1	16.41	3.91*
	Within	889.03	214-2=212	4.19	
	Total	1135.53	214		

* Indicates significant difference at 0.05 level.

** Indicates significant difference at 0.01 level.

Tab. F-Value at 0.05 = 3.89 and at 0.01 = 6.76.

and Marriage (6.79) were found to be significant as shown in Table 11. For rest of the films the effect of legal exposure was not significant which is evident from insignificant F-values. Thus, the null hypotheses is partially not accepted. It is accepted in case of films on Inheritance, Dowry and Divorce and not accepted for the films on Introduction, Marriage and Eve Teasing and Rape.

It is clear from Table 12, that there were significant differences in the gain score indicating gain in knowledge regarding "Women and Law", in each of the seven video films. This shows that there was considerable gain in knowledge for both the groups through the video films on "Women and Law". As evident from Table 12, the calculated t-values for pretest-posttest were found to be significant at 0.01 level of confidence.

Table 12

Distribution of the T-Ratio, Showing Significant Differences in Pretest-Posttest Scores of Respondents on the Seven Video Films in Relation to Legal Exposure of Family

Video Films	*Social Science Inclination*	X_1 *Pre-test*	X_2 *Post-test*	*Cal t Value*	*Tab. t Value 0.01*
Introduction	With Legal Exposure N = 54	12.40	15.66	8.76**	2.396
	Without N = 153	11.74	14.55	11.65**	2.352
Ive Teasing	With Legal Exposure N = 65	11.07	16.49	15.53**	2.390
	Without N = 160	11.14	15.86	23.86**	2.352
Inheritance	With Legal Exposure N = 52	13.63	17.17	9.84**	2.403
	Without N = 132	13.43	17.00	16.07**	2.358
Marriage	With Legal Exposure N = 57	12.08	18.08	13.96**	2.396
	Without N = 160	12.31	17.35	20.90**	2.352
Dowry	With Legal Exposure N = 67	11.50	16.29	14.50**	2.390
	Without N = 170	11.35	15.82	22.40**	2.352
Divorce	With Legal Exposure N = 62	11.30	16.70	15.06**	2.390
	Without N = 171	10.95	16.70	24.81**	2.352
Rape	With Legal Exposure N = 53	11.20	17.58	19.25**	2.403
	Without N = 162	11.01	16.87	27.89**	2.352

** Indicates significant difference at 0.01 level.

On the whole all the students have gained or learnt well after seeing all the video films on "Women and Law", as clearly seen in Table 12. The students have learnt significantly higher after seeing these 4 films namely, Introduction to Law, Eve-teasing Rape and Marriage. But the surprising fact in this finding is that students without legal exposure have scored higher than with legal exposure.

The reason for this could be that the legal exposure that is considered in this study could have happened long ago and perhaps the student was not directly exposed to it. This implies that we should not accept the students to come to the Faculty with legal exposure to know laws better. One can learn laws without being exposed to it in the past. Legal exposure of family is not a prerequisite to learn laws. On the whole legal awareness is not dependent on legal exposure of the family; one can build it at the preliminary stage by learning from such video films. Although we advocate that Personal Laws should be taught to young women, this sample showed that majority of the Home Science students came from such families which did not have legal exposure.

The implications from these findings are that knowledge of personal laws is equally benefited to all the students with or without their family's legal exposure. It is heartening to know one need not have parents, family members, neighbours who were involved in law suit to know law!

Social Work Background

In this section, the findings regarding the effectiveness of video films in relation to the social work background are reported.

It was found during the feasibility study that, among the informal sources family was found to be the most popular source of information about the law, followed by friends and neighbours. It is known that persuasive communication affects behaviour and thought process of an individual, and informal agents of communication and dissemination of knowledge, exert direct impact upon people. Family members, friends and neighbours were thought to be playing prominent role in making students aware of the provision of legal rights. When the hypothesis that there will be no significant difference in knowledge gain in terms of pre-post scores of the students according to the social work background was tested, the analysis revealed that all the seven calculated F-values for the films on "Women and Law", were not significant (Table 13). Meaning thereby that, there was no significant difference in the pretest and posttest scores of the students according to the social work background.

Table 13

ANCOVA, Showing Significance of Differences Scores After Removing the Effect of Pre Scores in the Knowledge by Learning Through the Video Films on "Women and Law" and the Social Work Background

Source of Variation-Films		*SS*	*DF*	*MSS*	*F Value*
Introduction	Treatment	0.03	2-1=1	0.03	0.008
	Within	989.59	206-2=204	4.83	
	Total	1359.05	206		
Eve Teasing	Treatment	1.59	2-1=1	1.59	0.48
	Within	728.83	224-2=222	3.28	
	Total	762.46	224		
Inheritance	Treatment	2.55	2-1=1	2.55	0.79
	Within	579.57	183-2=181	3.20	
	Total	667.45	183		
Marriage	Treatment	2.34	2-1=1	2.34	0.62
	Within	803.36	216-2=214	3.75	
	Total	835.83	216		
Dowry	Treatment	3.63	2-1=1	3.63	1.15
	Within	735.16	236-2=234	3.14	
	Total	778.65	236		
Divorce	Treatment	0.47	2-1=1	0.47	0.09
	Within	1137.85	232-2=230	4.94	
	Total	1262.56	232		
Rape	Treatment	1.41	2-1=1	1.41	0.33
	Within	904.03	214-2=212	4.26	
	Total	1135.53	214		

Hence, the hypothesis that there will be no significant difference in knowledge gain in terms of pre-post scores of the students according to the social work background was accepted. So it can be said that the social work background made no impact whatsoever, as far as knowledge about "Women and Law" is concerned.

As evident from Table 14, that all the seven t-values for the films on "Women and Law", were highly significant at 0.01

level of confidence. Meaning thereby that, there was significant difference in the pretest and posttest scores of the students.

Table 14
Distribution of the T-Ratio, Showing Significant Differences in Pretest-Posttest Scores of the Respondents on the Seven Video Films in Relation to Social Work Background

Video Films	*Social Work background*	X_1 *Pre-test*	X_2 *Post-test*	*Cal t Value*	*Tab. t Value 0.01*
Introduction	With S.W. N = 47	12.23	15.00	6.54**	2.412
	Without S.W. N = 160	11.82	14.80	12.82**	2.352
Eve Teasing	With S.W.N = 51	11.17	15.90	12.72**	2.403
	Without S.W. N = 174	11.10	16.09	25.26**	2.352
Inheritance	With S.W. N = 47	14.10	17.02	7.78**	2.412
	Without S.W. N = 137	13.28	17.06	17.54**	2.358
Marriage	With S.W. N = 59	12.23	17.71	13.29**	2.390
	Without S.W. N = 158	12.25	17.48	21.07**	2.352
Dowry	With S.W. N=57	11.26	16.15	16.49**	2.396
	Without S.W. N=180	11.44	15.90	21.83**	2.352
Divorce	With S.W. N = 57	11.33	16.70	13.52**	2.396
	Without S.W. N = 176	10.95	16.70	25.69**	2.352
Rape	With S.W. N = 53	11.69	17.43	14.76**	2.403
	Without S.W. N = 162	10.85	16.91	30.34**	2.352

** Indicates significant difference at 0.01 level.

Further examination of Table 14, shows that the mean scores indicated that the posttest scores increased after video teaching. This indicated that all the seven video films on "Women and Law", independently lead to increase in the knowledge level.

It is commonly presumed that family background experts impact on the mental horizon of the person. His or her world view is shaped to some extent, by his or her parents' occupation. It was assumed that the students who had social work background would gain more knowledge regarding "Women and Law". But this assumption did not hold true particularly in case of students' family's involvement in social work and knowledge gain regarding "Women and Law".

The small group of students who had such a social work background did not show any major difference in the gain of knowledge of any law. It should not be expected that majority of students should come from a family with social work background. All students with or without social work background benefitted from learning the content on "Women and Law".

Mother's Occupation

Table 15 and 16, reveal the effectiveness of video films in the teaching laws related to women and the variable "Mother's Occupation".

The findings of the feasibility study had indicated that mother's occupational status had significant relationship as far as the opinion towards legal education, as well as knowledge regarding various laws related to women, were concerned. This may be due to the fact that women play a pivotal force in every family. They shape the family and inculcate habits in their children. It has been known that education of mother means education of the family. If a mother is aware about her rights and duties, she will transmit the awareness to the family members more easily. It was assumed that status of mother's occupation will also affect the students' performance in learning the content on "Women and Law through video films.

The variation in gain in knowledge due to mother's occupation was computed by ANCOVA. The F-values in Table 15 show the variation in learning.

In Table 15, the findings revealed that respondents whose mothers were gainfully employed or were housewives both the groups of respondents equally benefitted through six video films on "Women and Law", as evident from insignificant F-values. The effect of mother's occupation was only significant for the film on Marriage as shown in Table 15. The significant difference in gain existed for the film on Marriage with F-value 7.06 which is significant at 0.01 level.

When the hypothesis that there will be no significant difference in knowledge gain in terms of pre-post scores of the students according to the Mother's occupation was tested, the data revealed that the calculated F-values were not significant for six video films on "Women and Law". However, for the film on 'Marriage[1], the F-value was significant. So, the null hypothesis was partially accepted, that is, accepted in case of the six video films, while not accepted in case of film on Marriage.

Table 15
ANCOVA, Showing Significance of Differences in the Post Scores After Removing the Effect of Pre Scores in the Knowledge by Learning Through the Video Films on "Women and Law" and the Mother's Occupation

Source of Variation-Film		*SS*	*DF*	*MSS*	*F Value*
Introduction	Treatment	12.18	2-1=1	12.18	2.55
	Within	974.44	206-2=204	4.77	
	Total	1359.05	206		
Eve Teasing	Treatment	0.74	2-1=1	0.74	0.22
	Within	729.68	224-2=222	3.28	
	Total	762.46	224		
Inheritance	Treatment	1.46	2-1=1	1.46	0.45
	Within	580.66	183-2=181	3.20	
	Total	667.45	183		
Marriage	Treatment	25.73	2-1=1	25.73	7.06**
	Within	779.97	216-2=214	3.64	
	Total	835.83	216		
Dowry	Treatment	0.001	2-1=1	0.001	0.00
	Within	738.79	236-2=234	3.15	
	Total	778.65	236		
Divorce	Treatment	0.88	2-1=1	0.88	0.17
	Within	1137.44	232-2=230	4.94	
	Total	1262.56	232		
Rape	Treatment	6.82	2-1=1	6.82	1.60
	Within	898.63	214-2=212	4.23	
	Total	1135.53	214		

**Indicates significant difference at 0.01 level.
Tab. F-Value at 0.05 = 3.89 and at 0.01 = 6.76

Table 15 further shows that the respondents did not differ significantly according to mother's occupation for learning content on different laws related to women. The difference due to mother's occupation was found only for learning the content on 'Marriage". As those respondents whose mothers were housewives they learnt much better the content on law for Marriage than those whose mothers were working. The reason for this could be the women who are merely housewives have the feeling of deprivation and later on they push their daughters for higher studies so that they are not exploited. We should not look down to the students whose mothers are housewives as they are more motivated to learn laws and particularly laws related to marriage. Marriage is a very common phenomenon which everyone has to face, whereas, help of other laws may not be needed by everyone.

Data were further analysed by computing paired t-tests to find out the exact differences in learning by the two categories of students according to Mother's Occupation. The Table 16 gives the differences in learning which is depicted in the form of t-values.

Table 16

Distribution of the T-Ratio,Showing Significant Differences in Pretest-Posttest Scores of Respondents on the Seven Video Films in Relation to Mother's Occupation

Video Films	*Mother's Occupation*	X_1 *Pre-test*	X_2 *Post-test*	*Cal t Value*	*Tab. t Value at 0.01*
Introduction	Employed N = 36	12.50	15.61	6.83**	2.434
	Housewife N = 171	11.79	14.68	12.74**	2.352
Eve Teasing	Employed N = 31	11.32	16.22	12.02**	2.453
	Housewife N = 194	11.09	16.09	25.75**	2.345
Inheritance	Employed N = 25	14.12	17.0	5.03**	2.485
	Housewife N = 159	13.39	17.06	18.51**	2.352
Marriage	Employed N = 34	12.61	16.79	7.71**	2.441
	Housewife N = 183	12.18	17.68	24.14**	2.352
Dowry	Employed N = 39	11.58	16.00	10.54**	2.426
	Housewife N = 198	11.36	15.95	24.48**	2.345
Divorce	Employed N = 37	11.56	16.70	10.85**	2.431
	Housewife N = 196	10.94	16.70	26.96**	2.345
Rape	Employed N = 34	11.61	16.85	11.93**	2.441
	Housewife N = 171	10.96	17.08	31.59**	2.352

** Indicates significant difference at 0.01 level.

It is clear from Table 16 that there were significant differences in the gain score indicating gain in knowledge regarding laws related to women through all the seven video films. This means that there was considerable gain in knowledge for all the groups through the video films on "Women and Law".

As the t-value was highly significant at 0.01 level for all the seven video films. Further re-examination of the Table revealed that the mean scores for posttest were significantly higher than the pretest scores. This means that the students' achievement differed significantly in the posttest.

Table 16 clearly shows that respondents have learnt significantly well through video films. However, for the film on 'Marriage' the respondents, whose mothers were housewives, have learnt better than those mothers were employed. The probable reason for this could be the students whose mothers are housewives must have heard their mothers complaining about their inability to take any action against injustice in the institute of marriage. Whereas respondents whose mothers were employed they possessed better awareness and knowledge. As they are gainfully employed it gave them exposure to the outer world. Hazarika (1991) explains that employment to some extent also changes a woman from her submissive behaviour to assertive behaviour with broader perspective of life.

The findings of a number of studies suggest that the mother's participation in the world of work has brought about structural and functional alterations in the family and marriage.

The findings confirmed the outcome of Sachidanand and Sinha (1984), where the result was more or less similar. They found that the better educated victims took to legal measures for solving their problems. Non-employed respondents had financial constraints which delayed their decisions in resolving the problems in married life. Contrary to this finding, small group of students who had working mothers, did not show gain of knowledge regarding personal laws.

In other words, it can be concluded from Tables 15 and 16, the presence and absence of mother's occupation had nothing to do with the knowledge gain. Hence, the subject "Women and Law", could be taught to the Home Science students regardless of the employment of their mothers.

Exposure to T.V./Video

Tabies 17 and 18, show the effectiveness of video films in relation to the Exposure of respondents to TV and Video.

The technology, whether it is television or video, properly supported and wisely employed, could help in meeting some of the most pressing educational needs of today. However, the production, approach and the treatment of the subject may vary. We must agree with Hills (1982, p. 45), when he says,

> "Educational technology should be seen not as the machine taking over the teacher's role, but rather in terms of a developing science of education which uses a host of methods, techniques and resources to assist the teacher and support the student in learning task."

Accepting the significance of educational television, Dale (1969, p. VII), rightly argues.

> "We must help students learn more, learn it faster, remember it better and apply it more effectively."

ANCOVA, was computed to determine variation due to the exposure to TV/Video and the knowledge gain regarding "Women and Law" through video films. F-values indicate such variation and are displayed in Table 17. Further probe into the findings of Table 17 revealed that respondents having high exposure or low exposure were equally benefitted through video films on "Women-and Law".

When the hypothesis that there will be no significant difference in knowledge gain in terms of pre-post scores of the students according to the TV/Video exposure was tested/ the data revealed that all the seven calculated F-values were not significant.

In the light of above findings the null hypothesis was accepted.

The applicability of the content might also help the women students in taking interest in the video films and gaining significant knowledge. The video films have been understood equally well by both the groups because the video films were prepared and presented in an understandable way. In other words, the students gained more or less the same amount of knowledge irrespective of their T.V./video exposure. It implies that we could teach Personal Laws to the students with low as well as high T.V./video exposure. Similar finding was reported by Gupta (1991). In her study video film was found equally effective by Home Science students having more or less exposure to television and video.

Table 17

ANCOVA, Showing Significance of Differences in the Post Scores After Removing the Effect of Pre Scores in the Knowledge by Learning Through the Video Films on "Women and Law", and Video/T.V. Exposure

Source of Variation-Film		*SS*	*DF*	*MSS*	*F Value*
Introduction	Treatment	4.02	2-1=1	4.02	0.83
	Within	982.60	206-2=204	4.81	
	Total	1359.05	206		
Eve Teasing	Treatment	0.10	2-1=1	0.10	0.03
	Within	730.32	224-2=222	3.29	
	Total	762.46	224		
Inheritance	Treatment	3.89	2-1=1	3.89	1.21
	Within	578.24	183-2=181	3.19	
	Total	667.45	183		
Marriage	Treatment	5.46	2-1=1	3.89	1.46
	Within	800.24	216-2=214	3.19	
	Total	835.83	216		
Dowry	Treatment	0.43	2-1=1	5.46	0.13
	Within	738.35	236-2=234	3.73	
	Total	778.65	236		
Divorce	Treatment	0.01	2-1=1	0.43	0.004
	Within	1138.30	232-2=230	3.15	
	Total	1262.56	232		
Rape	Treatment	7.31	2-1=1	0.01	1.72
	Within	898.13	214-2=212	4.94	
	Total	1135.53	214		

This finding regarding T.V./video exposure was also supported by Sachidanand and Sinha (1984). However, the sample in their study was the women from rural Gaya.

As discussed in Chapter 3 Methodology, respondents were divided into two categories of high and low exposure, on the basis of the total group mean of the T.V. Video viewing. The total group mean was found to be 18. All those respondents whose scores corresponded with the mean and above, were placed into high T.V. video viewing, and those who obtained scores which fell below the mean were categorised as less T.V. video viewing exposure.

Table 18
Distribution of the T-Ratio Showing Significant Differences in Pretest-Posttest Scores of the Respondents on the Seven Video Films in Relation to T.V./Video Exposure

Video Films	*T.V./Video Exposure*	X_1 *Pre-test*	X_2 *Post-test*	*Cal t Value*	*Tab. t Value 0.01*
Introduction	High Exposure N = 109	12.22	15.10	10.18**	2.364
	Low Exposure N = 98	11.58	14.56	10.18**	2.368
Eve Teasing	High Exposure N = 108	11.13	16.07	19.42**	2.364
	Low Exposure N = 117	11.11	16.02	20.51**	2.358
Inheritance	High Exposure N = 93	13.83	17.29	13.93**	2.368
	Low Exposure N = 91	13.14	16.81	12.85**	2.368
Marriage	High Exposure N=114	12.33	17.40	17.29**	2.364
	Low Exposure N = 103	12.16	17.69	18.05**	2.364
Dowry	High Exposure N = 118	11.51	16.02	19.40**	2.364
	Low Exposure N = 119	11.28	15.89	18.36**	2.358
Divorce	High Exposure N = 119	11.33	16.63	21.46**	2.358
	Low Exposure N = 114	10.74	16.63	19.79**	2.364
Rape	High Exposure N = 109	11.25	17.30	24.89**	2.364
	Low Exposure N = 106	10.86	16.78	22.54**	2.364

** Indicates significant difference at 0.01 level.

It is evident from the Table 18 that nearly equal number of respondents fell into the two categories of high and low exposure to T.V./Video.

The pretest scores of both the groups of students having low as well as high exposure to T.V./video scored nearly equal marks as evident from Table 18. The calculated t-value for pretest-posttest of all the seven video films and both the groups, with high and low exposure to T.V./video were found to be highly significant at 0.01 level of confidence. This means that the students' achievement differed significantly in the two tests.

As mentioned earlier, knowledge of law is relevant for todays' girls as they face eve-teasing, rape, violence and they are also aware of increasing rate of crime against women. So instead of the exposure to television and video, it may be a necessity for them to learn laws related to women.

The present finding was that although students were exposed to television and video, this kind of exposure did not help them to learn laws. The probable reason for this could be the kind of programmes which are seen on T.V. and video are mostly films, songs and entertainment programmes. Generally speaking, in India, T.V. and video are associated more with entertainment and less with education. So the students are more inclined to see T.V. and video for recreation and not so much for education. This could be a reason for the variable 'T.V./Video Exposure' to be insignificant in learning personal Laws.

It can be concluded from Tables 17 and 18, that each video film when shown separately for the two categories of students was found to be effective. On the whole, high as well as low media exposure made the respondents learnt significantly through all video films.

Socio-economic Status

This section presents the effectiveness of video films in relation to the Socio Economic Status. Data were analysed to check the variation in learning of the content "Women and Law", through video films due to the Socio-Economic Status of the respondents. The Table 19A, shows in general the difference due to the Socio Economic Status which is shown in form of calculated F-values in Table 19A.

The hypothesis stated that there will be no significant difference in knowledge gain in terms of pre-post scores of the students according to the Socio-Economic Status and was tested by applying ANCOVA. The results of ANCOVA, showed that the Socio-Economic Status played a significant role in learning of the content on "Women and Law", through the films namely Introduction, Marriage, Dowry and Rape as the significant F-values depicts in Table 19A.

Hence the null hypothesis was partially accepted in case of Eve-teasing, Inheritance and Divorce as the Socio Economic Status did not play its role in learning the content. However, the hypothesis was not accepted in case of learning the content on Introduction to Law, Marriage, Dowry and Rape.

Table 19A

ANCOVA Showing Significance of Differences in the Poet Scores After Removing the Effect of Pre Scores in the Knowledge by Learning Through the Video Films on "Women and Law" and the Socio-Economic Status

Source of Variation-Film		*SS*	*DF*	*MSS*	*F Value*
Introduction	Treatment	37.48	2-1=1	18.74	4.00*
	Within	949.14	206-2=204	4.67	
	Total	1359.05	206		
Eve Teasing	Treatment	13.93	2-1=1	6.96	2.14
	Within	716.50	224-2=222	3.24	
	Total	762.46	224		
Inheritance	Treatment	12.82	2-1=1	6.41	2.02
	Within	569.30	183-2=181	3.16	
	Total	667.45	183		
Marriage	Treatment	40.81	2-1=1	20.40	5.68*
	Within	764.89	216-2=214	3.59	
	Total	835.83	216		
Dowry	Treatment	41.61	2-1=1	20.80	6.95*
	Within	697.17	236-2=234	2.99	
	Total	778.65	236		
Divorce	Treatment	6.94	2-1=1	3.47	0.703
	Within	1131.38	232-2=230	4.94	
	Total	1262.56	232		
Rape	Treatment	98.44	2-1=1	49.22	12.87**
	Within	807.00	214-2=212	3.82	
	Total	1135.53	214		

* Indicates significant difference at 0.05 level.
*Indicates significant difference at 0.01 level.
Tab. F-Value at 0.05 = 3.83 and at 0.01 = 6.76

Through the preliminary analysis it was found that Socio Economic Status made its impact in learning the content of Introduction to Law, Marriage, Divorce and Rape as reported in Table 19A. Further analysis was done to find out, out of the three groups of SES which group learnt significantly different than the other, data were further analysed by computing ANCOVA, which are presented in Table 19-B.

Examination of the Table 19-B, shows the calculated F-value of high socio-economic status group differed significantly from group of low socio economic status, while learning the content on Dowry. The calculated F value of respondents from high socio economic status were found to be significant at 0.05 level of confidence for the film on Dowry.

Table 19B

ANCOVA, Showing Significance of Differences in the Knowledge by Learning Through the Four Video Films and the Socio-Economic Groups

Source of Variation-Film		*SS*	*DF*	*MSS*	*F Value*
Introduction					
High Vs. Middle SES	Treatment	18.63	1	83.63	
	Within	944.78	196	4.82	3.86
Middle Vs. Low SES					
	Treatment	7.05	1	7.05	
	Within	309.26	60	5.15	1.36
High Vs. Low SES	Treatment	23.17	1	23.17	
	Within	637.30	149	157.70	5.41*
Marriage					
High Vs. Middle SES	Treatment	3.25	1	3.25	
	Within	525.76	151	3.48	0.39
Middle Vs. Low SES	Treatment	28.99	1	28.99	
	Within	209.55	44	4.76	6.08*
High Vs. Low SES	Treatment	41.32	1	41.32	
	Within	340.17	118	2.88	14.33*
Dowry					
High Vs. Middle SES	Treatment	10.79	1	10.79	
	Within	478.77	171	2.80	3.85
Middle Vs. Low SES	Treatment	5.95	1	5.95	
	Within	127.56	52	2.45	2.42
High Vs. Low SES	Treatment	16.83	1	16.83	
	Within	373.30	132	2.82	5.95*
Rape					
High Vs. Middle SES	Treatment	31.47	1	31.47	
	Within	486.12	150	3.20	9.83**
Middle Vs. Low SES	Treatment	49.12	1	49.12	
	Within	347.61	49	7.09	6.92**
High Vs. Low SES	Treatment	96.95	1	96.95	
	Within	455.85	112	4.07	23.81**

* Indicates significant difference at 0.05 level

**Indicates significant difference at 0.01 level

Tab F value at 44 d.f. 0.05 level = 4.06 at 50 d.f. 0.05 level = 4.03
at 112 d.f. 0.01 level = 6.90 at 125 d.f. 0.05 level = 3.92
at 125 d.f. 0.01 level = 6.84 at 150 d.f. 0.05 level = 3.91
at 150 d.f. 0.01 level = 9.83

The reason for this could be that the upper and middle class parents tend to have higher aspiration for their daughters than the lower class. Thus, the daughters may have higher aspirations either as a result of pressure from the parents or as a result of internalising parental pressures or both. In a society with a tradition of upward mobility, the students from Middle income group tend to aspire for higher status. This could be the reason why the high and middle socio economic status students learnt maximum on the content on Marriage and Dowry which involves money matters.

To find out the exact differences in the pre-post tests due to the Socio-Economic Status of the respondents the data were further analysed by computing Paired t-tests. Table 20, gives details of the results of t-tests. The differences of the pre-post tests of the three different Socio Economic groups can be seen in the form of calculated t-values.

The findings regarding SES variable revealed that a large per cent of the respondents fell in two categories of socio-economic status, namely, upper and middle class. The students are greatly affected by the family's financial and social position. People from various socio-economic status look at the different aspects of life in different manners. Table 20, shows that amongst the three categories of socio-economic status, the respondents from the upper and middle strata of the socio-economic status were found to be having higher mean scores for pretest as well as posttest than the respondents from the lower socio-economic class.

Table 20, shows that all the 7 calculated t-values for students from different socio-economic groups were found to be highly significant at 0.01 level of confidence. Further examination of the mean scores indicated that the pretest scores of all the three socio-economic groups for all the seven video films increased significantly during posttest. This leads to conclude that all the video films were effective in increasing the knowledge regarding "Women and Law", in context of respondents' socio-economic status.

Table 20
Distribution of the T-Ratio, Showing Significant Differences in Pretest-Posttest Scores of Respondents on the Seven Video Films in Relation to Socio Economic Status

Video Films	*Socio Economic Status*	X_1 *Pre-test*	X_2 *Post-test*	*Cal t Value*	*Tab. t Value 0.01*
Introduction	High N = 144	12.14	15.18	13.14**	2.358
	Middle N = 55	11.30	14.16	6.25**	2.396
	Low N = 8	12.00	13.37	2.58*	2.89
Eve Teasing	High N = 153	11.27	16.24	24.19**	2.352
	Middle N = 62	10.77	15.66	14.88**	2.390
	Low N = 10	11.00	15.50	3.68**	2.764
Inheritance	High N = 127	13.70	17.26	15.58**	2.358
	Middle N = 50	13.26	16.56	9.93**	2.403
	Low N = 7	11.28	16.71	4.48**	2.998
Marriage	High N = 156	12.17	17.76	23.32**	2.352
	Middle N = 51	12.37	17.13	10.62**	2.403
	Low N = 10	12.80	16.10	2.68	2.764
Dowry	High N = 165	11.41	16.23	25.33**	2.352
	Middle N = 62	11.37	15.38	10.56**	2.390
	Low N = 10	11.40	15.00	4.26**	2.764
Divorce	High N = 160	11.24	16.78	23.29**	2.352
	Middle N = 63	10.60	16.65	16.56**	2.390
	Low N = 10	10.70	15.80	5.45**	2.764
Rape	High N = 148	11.34	17.54	30.70**	2.352
	Middle N = 58	10.74	16.27	14.43**	2.396
	Low N = 9	8.55	13.77	5.56**	2.821

** Indicates significant at 0.01 level.
Tab t value at 0.05 = 1.86 at df 8

Table 20, further shows that video films on Rape and Marriage were found to be most effective for the students of high socio-economic group t-value 30.70 and 25.33 respectively. Interestingly the same film on Marriage was found to be least effective by the students from low socio-economic status with t-value 2.68.

The findings regarding socio-economic status. Table 19 and 20, revealed that the respondents of high socio-economic status gained more knowledge with the use of video films. The respondents of high socio-economic status, are usually exposed to many novel experiences, such as movies, television, video and various others, because of their high socio economic status, whereas low socio-economic status are deprived of these things and are usually not very familiar with them. On the whole, video films were found to be effective with all the three groups in imparting knowledge on "Women and Law". However, video films were found more effective with students from high socio-economic group.

The video films on Eve-teasing, Inheritance and Divorce were not affected by the students socio-economic status as is evident by insignificant F-value. The reason for this could be these problems are becoming very common in todays world and it does not matter which socio economic status one may belong to.

Modernity

This section comprises of findings related to the effectiveness of video films in relation to the modernity. It was assumed that the learning of laws may be affected by the level of modernity because a modern student would prefer to use the laws for her benefit. A modern student may be disposed to new ideas and new ways of thinking and acting. She may take to certain things easily that are taught during the study programme while a conservative student may not accept the same thing because she is not ready to change and she may show less interest.

ANCOVA, was computed to determine the variation in the modernity of the students and gain in knowledge. The F-value indicates such variation in Table 21. Further probe into the findings of Table 21, show that modern as well as conservative students equally benefitted through video films on "Women and Law". This implies that in todays' world, where crime rate against women is increasing, the women students of Faculty of Home Science, whether they are Modern or Conservative, they feel it is necessary to learn and know about personal laws related to women, so that they can be useful to them in the time of crisis.

The data revealed that all the seven calculated F-values were insignificant. That means the variable of Modernity, did not make any difference in learning laws. Hence, the hypothesis that there will be no significant difference in knowledge gain in terms of pre-post scores of the students according to the overall modernity was accepted.

Table 21

ANCOVA, Showing Significance of Differences in the Post Scores After Removing the Effect of Pre Scores in the Knowledge by Learning Through the Video Films on "Women and Law", and Modernity

Source of Variation-Film		*SS*	*DF*	*MSS*	*F Value*
Introduction	Treatment	3.58	2-1=1	3.58	0.74
	Within	983.04	206-2=204	4.81	
	Total	1359.05	206		
Eve Teasing	Treatment	1.53	2-1=1	1.53	0.46
	Within	728.89	224-2=222	3.28	
	Total	762.46	224		
Inheritance	Treatment	0.25	2-1=1	0.25	0.07
	Within	581.88	183-2=181	3.21	
	Total	667.45	183		
Marriage	Treatment	0.55	2-1=1	1.58	0.14
	Within	805.15	216-2=214	3.15	
	Total	835.83	216		
Dowry	Treatment	1.58	2-1=1	3.16	0.50
	Within	737.20	236-2=234	4.93	
	Total	778.65	236		
Divorce	Treatment	3.16	2-1=1	0.87	0.64
	Within	1135.16	232-2=230	4.26	
	Total	1262.56	232		
Rape	Treatment	0.87	2-1=1	49.22	0.20
	Within	904.57	214-2=212	3.82	
	Total	1135.53	214		

Table 22, further shows the exact differences in learning the content on "Women and Law", due to the level of modernity of the respondents. These differences are computed in the form of t-tests and are depicted by calculated t-values in Table 22.

Table 22
Distribution of the T-Ratio, Showing Significant Differences in Pretest-Posttest Scores of Respondents on the Seven Video Films in Relation to Modernity

Video Films	*Modernity*	X_1 *Pre-test*	X_2 *Post-test*	*Cal t Value*	*Tab. t 0.01*
Introduction	Modern N = 164	12.20	15.03	12.78**	2.352
	Conservative N = 43	10.81	14.13	6.70**	2.423
Eve Teasing	Modern N = 180	11.15	16.09	26.82**	2.352
	Conservative N = 45	11.02	15.86	10.40**	2.412
Inheritance	Modern N = 145	13.75	17.14	16.49**	2.352
	Conservative N = 39	12.51	16.71	9.44**	2.426
Marriage	Modern N = 178	12.38	17.58	21.48**	2.352
	Conservative N = 39	11.66	17.35	13.85**	2.426
Dowry	Modern N = 198	11.43	16.00	24.20**	2.345
	Conservative N = 39	11.20	15.74	11.19**	2.426
Divorce	Modern N = 192	11.33	16.83	26.22**	2.345
	Conservative N = 41	9.70	16.09	12.75**	2.423
Rape	Modern N=178	11.17	17.11	31.09**	2.352
	Conservative N = 37	10.54	16.70	12.79**	2.431

**Indicates significant difference at 0.01 level.

As discussed in Chapter 3 Methodology, the respondents were categorised on the basis of their summated scores on Alex Inkle's standardized scale. It is seen from Table 22, that high percentage of the respondents were modern according to the Alex Inkle's standardized scale of adaptation to modernity.

As evident from Table 22, the pretest scores of both the groups of Modern as well as conservative scored nearly equal marks as evident from the Table 22. However, after the video teaching, the students who were modern gained more in comparison to the students who were conservative as indicated by their higher posttest mean scores in all the seven video films on "Women and Law".

As shown in Table 22, the calculated t-value for pretest-posttest of all the seven video films and both the groups, were found to be highly significant at 0.01 level of confidence. This means that the students' achievement differed significantly in the two tests.

Further analysis of t-value indicates that film on Rape (31.09), Divorce (26.22) and Eve-teasing (26.82) were most effective for the modern students.

This indicated that all the seven video films on "Women and Law", independently lead to increase in the knowledge. To conclude it can be said, that a higher percentage of the respondents were modern rather than conservative. The reason for this finding could again be because, Baroda has become a cosmopolitan city people are exposed to various kinds of life patterns.

Since, the Home Science girls have been exposed to the new life styles, most of them becoming modern rather than remaining conservative.

Modern as well as conservative students understand the social significance and the necessity of learning laws. Therefore, the respondents must have felt the need to learn the laws related to women. You may be just what you are and you will be able to learn law. That means what ever type of life style you adopt either modern or conservative, no type is superior to other for learning the laws related to women.

Personality

This section presents the effectiveness of video films in relation to Personality of the respondents.

The impact of video films on students may also be influenced by their personality. The typical extroverts are flexible and socially adaptable, good at speech and are free from worries. In contrast, introverts are socially shy, like to work alone, are less flexible, better at writing and inclined to worries. Therefore, the different personality dimensions of students may affect the way they react to various aspects included in video films on "Women and Law".

The standardized Extroversion-Introversion Inventory developed by V.S. Shanthamani and A. Hafeez, (1974) was used for categorising the students according to their personality.

When the hypothesis that there will be no significant difference in knowledge gain in terms of pre-post scores of the students according to their personality was tested, the data revealed that all the calculated F-values for the seven video films on "Women and Law", were insignificant. Hence the null hypothesis was accepted. This F-value indicates no significant difference in the knowledge gain among the students having different personality dimensions, as seen in Table 23.

Table 23

ANCOVA, Showing Significance of Differences in the Post Scores After Removing the Effect of Pre Scores in the-Knowledge by Learning Through the Video Films on "Women and Law", and the Personality of the Students

Source of Variation-Film		*SS*	*DF*	*MSS*	*F Value*
Introduction	Treatment	4.38	2-1=1	2.19	0.45
	Within	982.24	206-2=204	4.83	
	Total	1359.05	206		
Eve Teasing	Treatment	2.53	2-1=1	1.26	0.38
	Within	727.89	224-2=222	3.29	
	Total	762.46	224		
Inheritance	Treatment	5.46	2-1=1	2.73	0.85
	Within	576.66	183-2=181	3.20	
	Total	667.45	183		
Marriage	Treatment	8.55	2-1=1	4.27	1.14
	Within	797.16	216-2=214	3.74	
	Total	835.83	216		
Dowry	Treatment	8.38	2-1=1	4.19	1.33
	Within	730.40	236-2=234	3.13	
	Total	778.65	236		
Divorce	Treatment	4.98	2-1=1	2.49	0.50
	Within	1133.34	232-2=230	4.94	
	Total	1262.56	232		
Rape	Treatment	15.33	2-1=1	15.33	1.81
	Within	890.11	214-2=212	4.21	
	Total	1135.53	214		

So it can be said that personality of the student made no impact whatsoever as far as knowledge about "Women and Law" is concerned. Similar findings were reported by Kundu (1980). She reported that there was a statistically insignificant relationship between the academic achievement and the personality of the students.

As revealed in Table 24, the percentages of extrovert students were highest for all the seven films followed by ambivert and introvert. It is good that among the First Year class there are more extroverts than introverts.

Table 24

Distribution of the T-Ratio, Showing Significant Differences in Pretest-Posttest Scores of Respondents on the Seven Video Films in Relation to Personality

Video Films	*Personality*	X_1 *Pre-test*	X_2 *Post-test*	*Cal t Value*	*Tab. t 0.01*
Introduction	Introvert N = 31	12.00	17.22	10.55**	2.441
	Ambivert N = 82	12.24	17.39	13.19**	2.381
	Extrovert N = 94	12.34	17.75	18.49**	2.364
Eve Teasing	Introvert N = 37	11.05	15.89	11.37**	2.434
	Ambivert N = 81	11.22	15.98	16.41**	2.374
	Extrovert N = 107	11.07	16.14	19.96**	2.364
Inheritance	Introvert N = 29	13.89	16.79	6.96**	2.467
	Ambivert N = 67	13.32	17.00	10.98**	2.390
	Extrovert N = 88	13.48	17.18	13.85**	2.374
Marriage	Introvert N = 35	12.00	17.22	10.55**	2.441
	Ambivert N = 74	12.24	17.39	13.19**	2.381
	Extrovert N = 108	12.34	17.75	18.49**	2.364
Dowry	Introvert N = 38	11.86	15.63	7.58**	2.431
	Ambivert N = 87	11.41	15.97	17.14**	2.374
	Extrovert N = 112	11.24	16.06	20.03**	2.364
Divorce	Introvert N = 36	11.30	16.47	9.27**	2.438
	Ambivert N = 84	11.00	16.83	19.76**	2.374
	Extrovert N = 113	11.00	16.68	19.80**	2.364
Rape	Introvert N = 39	11.02	16.48	11.15**	2.429
	Ambivert N = 76	11.05	17.06	21.33**	2.381
	Extrovert N = 100	11.09	17.25	24.24**	2.364

** Indicates significant difference at 0.01 level.

The ambivert gives evidence of behaviour that may be extrovert, in some situation and introvert in others. For example, a person may be friendly but likes to work alone. Most of the people belong to the ambivert group. The Home Science students did not show this normal trend.

The mean scores of pretest revealed that the students with Extrovert personality had better knowledge than Ambiverts and Introverts. The analysis of the post test scores also showed the similar trend. Overall difference in the achievement of students according to the personality was found to be highly significant as indicated by value of t. The video films were found to be very effective as students learnt the content on "Women and Law", irrespective of their personality. However, comparatively Extroverts have learnt better than Introverts and Ambiverts. Similar findings were reported by Kausal (1986), who studied the impact of television viewing on the respondents with varying personality dimensions in terms of gain in knowledge. Findings were that introverts learnt more about social problems like 'inequality of sexes' whereas extroverts learnt more about legal problems like 'divorce' and 'dowry'.

Although it is theorised and psychologists have found that introverts learn best but in this study reverse is true. Comparatively speaking, extroverts have learnt about laws better than the introverts. So, students should be taught and helped to be extroverts as being introvert hinders learning of laws.

Level of Academic Achievement

It can be clearly seen from Tables 25 and 26, the effectiveness of video films in relation to Academic Achievement. To find out the variation in learning of the content on "Women and Law", through video films due to the level of Academic Achievement, ANCOVA was computed. The F-value, depicts such variation in Table 25.

It was surprising to note in Table 25, that the high achievers as well as low achievers earned almost similar scores. As the high achievers did not score significantly higher in comparison to the low achievers which is evident from all the seven insignificant F-values.

The hypothesis stating that no significant difference in knowledge gain in terms of pre-post scores of the students according to level of academic achievement was accepted. As it was found that effect of previous academic achievement on the overall knowledge gain was not significant as revealed in Table 25.

Table 25

ANCOVA, Showing Significance of Differences in the Post Scores After Removing the Effect of Pre Scores in the Knowledge by Learning Through the Video Films on "Women and Law", and Academic Achievement

Source of Variation-Film		*SS*	*DF*	*MSS*	*F Value*
Introduction	Treatment	7.19	2-1=1	7.19	1.49
	Within	979.43	206-2=204	4.80	
	Total	1359.05	206		
Eve Teasing	Treatment	8.42	2-1=1	8.42	2.58
	Within	722.01	224-2=222	3.25	
	Total	762.46	224		
Inheritance	Treatment	0.02	2-1=1	0.02	0.01
	Within	582.10	183-2=181	3.21	
	Total	667.45	183		
Marriage	Treatment	5.97	2-1=1	5.97	1.59
	Within	799.73	216-2=214	3.73	
	Total	835.83	216		
Dowry	Treatment	5.70	2-1=1	5.70	1.82
	Within	733.08	236-2=234	3.13	
	Total	778.65	236		
Divorce	Treatment	6.27	2-1=1	6.27	1.27
	Within	1132.04	232-2=230	4.92	
	Total	1162.56	232		
Rape	Treatment	3.89	2-1=1	3.89	1.27
	Within	901.55	214-2=212	4.25	
	Total	1135.53	214		

The researcher's main objective was to reach to the average Home Science student. That is, to teach content on "Women and Law", to the students of both the groups of high achievers as well as low achievers, in other words, all the average students. The findings of Table 25 also show that all the 7 video films have appealed to both the groups of students having high level of academic achievement as well as low level of academic achievement.

The video films were made, it seems keeping the average learner in mind, may be this could be the reason why a significant difference between the high achievers and low achievers is not found.

The data were further analysed to find out the difference in gain by applying paired t and the calculated t-values are presented in Table 26.

Table 26

Distribution of the T-Ratio, Showing Significant Differences in Pretest-Posttest Scores of Respondents on the Seven Video Films in Relation to Academic Achievement

Films	*Academic Achievement*	X_1 *Pre-test*	X_2 *Post-test*	*Cal t Value*	*Tab. t 0.01*
Introduction	Low Achievers (N = 115)	11.89	14.66	11.79**	2.364
	High Achievers (N = 92)	11.94	15.06	8.91**	2.368
Eve Teasing	Low Achievers (N = 120)	11.06	15.85	20.27**	2.364
	High Achievers (N = 105)	11.19	16.26	19.72**	2.364
Inheritance	Low Achievers (N = 99)	13.48	17.04	13.21**	2.364
	High Achievers (N = 85)	13.50	17.07	13.57**	2.374
Marriage	Low Achievers (N = 120)	12.13	17.38	18.01**	2.358
	High Achievers (N = 96)	12.40	17.75	17.27**	2.368
Dowry	Low Achievers (N = 128)	11.27	15.79	18.39**	2.358
	High Achievers (N = 109)	11.55	16.15	19.63**	2.364
Divorce	Low Achievers (N = 125)	11.16	16.58	19.85**	2.358
	High Achievers (N = 108)	10.90	16.84	21.48**	2.364
Rape	Low Achievers (N = 114)	11.15	16.95	22.98**	2.364
	High Achievers (N = 101)	10.96	17.14	24.71**	2.364

** Indicates significant difference at 0.01 level.

As seen in Table 26, mean scores of pretest indicated that high achievers had slightly higher mean scores than the low achievers which was not significant.

Similar trend was found for the mean of posttest scores. The high achievers' scores were higher than the low achievers' except for films on Eve teasing, Marriage and Introduction. Low achievers gained more knowledge in the films on Eve teasing, Marriage and Introduction. These films had rich experiences like drama and more visuals in comparison to other video films. This clearly indicates that low achievers were helped by the use of more senses, more details and more illustration to grasp the concept regarding "Women and Law".

Findings regarding academic achievement revealed that high achievers gained more knowledge when taught with simple lecture form in video i.e. films on Divorce and Rape. This clearly shows that high achievers with their high mental ability, must have been able to grasp concepts, with visual and verbal symbols. The higher mean scores of high achievers indicated that high achievers had higher gain in knowledge as compared to low achievers. The reason for this could be that students who do well academically are intellectually superior. They may be more aware and better oriented, compared to low achievers. Hence, they tend to be better motivated than the low achievers.

Table 26, further reveals that all the seven video films were found to be very effective for low achievers as well as high achievers. The difference between the pre-posttest scores of both the groups was very significant as indicated by t-value. Video teaching of law, was found interesting and effective, by the low as well as high achievers.

To conclude, it can be said that uniformly no significant difference between the high achievers and low achievers was established, indicating that all the 7 video films are equally good for high achievers and low achievers. As the course "Women and Law", is planned to be more knowledge oriented, it was advisable to use persuasive method, with a lot of illustrations and real life situations, as it is done in film on Introduction, Divorce and Marriage.

The previous academic achievement did not significantly affect the gain in knowledge regarding the content on "Women and Law". It would not be proper to divide the instructional groups on the basis of achievement. If it is done, there will be no interaction between low achievers and high achievers. The low achievers may not be motivated to progress or improve because they would lack the exposure to good quality work.

The teacher must be conscious of their expectations of low achievers. The teachers must know that the less bright student can not learn all that the bright ones can learn.

Taking a realistic view and considering the preliminary level for which the course is planned, the administrators and the teachers may be satisfied with this trend of student performance. The performance indicating gain in knowledge can be considered satisfactory for the undergraduates.

English Competence

In this section finding related to effectiveness of video films in relation to English competence is presented.

To find out the variation in learning due to the competence in English, ANCOVA was computed. The F-values in Table 27 shows the variation. Table 27 reveals the effect of English competence.

The effect of English competence was found to be maximum for the video films on Inheritance and Divorce. The respondents having high English competence gained significantly higher scores than their counterparts. The reason could be that the content of these two films were delivered through lecture method which were in English and the students having low English competence must have found it difficult to grasp and understand them.

The null hypothesis stating that there will be no significant difference in the knowledge gain, in terms of pre-post scores of the students according to the English competence was not accepted, as the effect of English competence was found to be highly significant. Table 27.

F-value being significant for competence in English showed that in all the seven films the students with high competence achieved significantly higher scores compared to the students with low competence.

Table 27

ANCOVA, Showing Significance of Differences in the Post Scores After Removing the Effect of Pre Scores in the Knowledge by Learning Through the Video Films on "Women and Law", and the English Competence

Source of Variation-Film		*SS*	*DF*	*MSS*	*F Value*
Introduction	Treatment	51.71	2-1=1	51.71	11.28**
	Within	934.91	206-2=204	4.58	
	Total	1359.05	206		
Eve Teasing	Treatment	99.01	2-1=1	99.01	34.81**
	Within	631.41	224-2=222	2.84	
	Total	764.46	224		
Inheritance	Treatment	136.93	2-1=1	136.93	55.67**
	Within	445.19	183-2=181	2.46	
	Total	665.45	183		
Marriage	Treatment	67.61	2-1=1	67.61	19.60**
	Within	738.09	216-2=214	3.44	
	Total	835.83	216		
Dowry	Treatment	91.76	2-1=1	91.76	33.18**
	Within	647.02	236-2=234	2.76	
	Total	778.65	236		
Divorce	Treatment	210.36	2-1=1	210.36	52.14**
	Within	927.96	232-2=230	4.03	
	Total	1262.56	232		
Rape	Treatment	113.42	2-1=1	113.42	30.35**
	Within	792.02	214-2=212	3.73	
	Total	1135.53	214		

**Indicates significant difference at 0.01 level.
Tab. F-value at 0.01 = 6.76

Table 27, further shows that the video films on Marriage and Dowry which had some part of it in Gujarati, the F value was not as large as film on Inheritance which was completely in English. This implies that if the video method is to be used for teaching, lot of visual aids, illustrations and main points should be emphasized, so that even students with low English competence can comprehend, as was seer in the case of film on Rape and Eve-testing.

The competence in English was found to be having a differential impact on students' achievement in relation to the video films.

According to Bloom is it a part of the name? Because *et al* means etc, in other words (1971), verbal ability and language competence are significantly related to the achievement in the majority of the subjects. This finding confirms the outcome of other studies where the results were similar. Menon (1984), and Joshi (1987) found positive correlation between English competence and learning through multimedia strategy. Mandal (1992), found students with good English language competence had better scores as compared to the respondents with poor English language competence while studying in college.

To find out the exact differences in the gain in knowledge about "Women and Law", due to the variable Competence in English, paired t-tests were computed. The differences are depicted in the form of Calculated t values in Table 28.

Table 28

Distribution of the T-Ratio, Showing Significant Differences in Pretest-Posttest Scores of Respondents on the Seven Video Films in Relation to English Competence

Films	*Academic Achievement*	X_1 *Pre-test*	X_2 *Post-test*	*Cal t Value*	*Tab. t 0.01*
Introduction	Low Competence (N = 84)	10.44	13.67	9.11**	2.374
	High Competence (N = 123)	12.92	15.64	11.32**	2.358
Eve Teasing	Low Competence (N = 90)	10.88	15.20	14.25**	2.368
	High Competence (N = 135)	11.28	16.61	26.44**	2.358
Inheritance	Low Competence (N = 63)	13.11	15.76	8.75**	2.390
	High Competence (N = 121)	13.69	17.72	17.65**	2.358
Marriage	Low Competence (N = 78)	11.91	16.75	12.56**	2.381
	High Competence (N = 139)	12.44	17.98	22.25**	2.358
Dowry	Low Competence (N = 97)	11.41	15.21	14.00**	2.368
	High Competence (N = 140)	11.39	16.47	24.32**	2.358
Divorce	Low Competence (N = 99)	10.38	15.44	15.49**	2.364
	High Competence (N = 134)	11.53	17.63	26.33**	2.358
Rape	Low Competence (N = 87)	10.58	15.98	18.40**	2.374
	High Competence (N = 128)	11.39	17.76	29.33**	2.358

**Indicates significant difference at 0.01 level.

Table 28, shows that there were more students in the category of High Competence in comparison to the students from Low Competence.

The first year semester grade of English subject in the academic year (1992-93), was considered to be an indicator of their level of English competence.

The analysis of Table 28 shows that students with high competence in English-achieved higher compared to the students with low competence in English, although both the groups achieved significantly.

As evident from the Table 28, the calculated 't' value of pretest-posttest were found to be significant at 0.01 level of confidence for the respondents. This indicated that the mean scores of pretest-posttest differed significantly.

Further examination of Table revealed that, mean scores of post test were significantly higher than the mean scores of pretest, which indicated gain in knowledge due to English competence on "Women and Law". Students having high English competence gained more knowledge through video films, in comparison to the students with low English competence.

Table 28, shows that respondents gained significant knowledge through video films irrespective of their English-competence (t-value). However, students from high English competence group, gained significantly higher than the low English competence.

The students with low and high competence in English both learnt well through video. However, higher English competence definitely learnt better. It can be inferred that English competence allows higher level of learning through video films which are in English. If only traditional method of lecturing is used, the students with low competence will have difficulty in learning. Therefore, every possible course at undergraduate level should be supplemented with video teaching. Most of the time teachers are worried about the students with poor English competence and if students are taught with video they can perhaps compete with good students.

According to Mandal (1992) students should be helped to acquire good English language competence at school level. The students coming from vernacular medium suffer the most and it is not possible to improve English at the college level.

CONCLUSIONS AND IMPLICATIONS BASED ON FINDINGS

In order to use video films in teaching a course "Women and Law", certain conclusions can be drawn on the basis of the findings of the present study. It is difficult to conclude with maximum certainty on the basis of this study because it is the first study of its kind, and has built-in limitations of the sample and the nature of the experiment.

It can be said from this first multidimensional study, that the developed outline of the course "Women and Law" is learnable and acceptable by students and yet there is a wide scope for its expansion. The course outline was developed logically as a 'Model' was adopted to develop the course and precautions were taken to assure that no psychological gaps in learning will occurs, As this was the first attempt, the content was deliberately simplified arid the evaluation of learning was also simple. May be later on some advanced course can be planned.

However, it can be concluded from the present findings that the detailed outline of a course "Women and Law", was feasible for learning as there was apparent gain in knowledge of the students after viewing the video films based on such a course outline. The trends of findings of quasi-experiment further supported learning theories which postulate that the increased reinforcement, recapitulation, cumulative sequence, and psychological arrangement of the topics enhance learning, as a significant gain in knowledge was found for all the seven video films on "Women and Law". Therefore, it can be concluded that well balanced and systematically organized films can be produced by teachers. The teachers should be encouraged to use such video films for teaching instead of lectures alone.

As the films tried to include most of the required teaching resources which are not always possible in the class room situation, they added to the clarity and understanding regarding the topic. For example, the 'Drama' shown in the video film may not be brought to the classroom in the live situation. Thus, video films tried to overcome the limitations of a lecture method and thereby helping the students to gain more knowledge. It is said, 'seeing is believing' and these videos have visuals with the commentary on the subject matter, to illustrate this principle. Illustration and motion in the video films held the attention of the learners and helped to score high in the knowledge test.

Considering the wider and modern concept of the Home Science Education, the course on law becomes very much a part of its content. Therefore, teaching laws through video films will prove very useful in Home Science colleges.

The delivery of content through the video films was direct, simple, open, down to earth, which facilitated learning of law. The entire positive findings can be attributed to ease, simplicity and directness of the video films. Along with this finding, the investigator took great care of making everybody comfortably seated while viewing. The whole class was divided into small groups, close to the video which helped the students in internalizing the content.

The laws which were selected were for young women regardless of their characteristics. The teaching of laws through seven video films concretely showed that women need to know these laws related to women. However, significant differences were found in the gain in knowledge regarding "Women and Law", in relation to stream of study, medium of instruction, social science inclination, and English competence. Thus, these variables were found to be very relevant. Although some other variables were relevant from a social point of view, very small portions of the sample were having variables namely, Legal Exposure, Social work background and place of residence. The effect of these variables could not be found because the sample size was very small. It is also possible to describe and operationally define these variables in a totally different manner in a future study, and to discover about their relation to learning of laws.

On the other hand, there may be some other variables which could help in learning of law. The Home Science students perceive the need to learn laws related to women. Perhaps today's college students face situations of crimes against women like disregard of property rights, marriage and divorce problem. Therefore, their sensitivity to learn laws could have developed. The present students thus, can be considered more motivated to learn laws. It is the prime time for them to be taught laws. The need to become more independent, more self protective and more knowledgeable, seems to have developed in college students. Therefore, it is justified to teach laws.

In the video films the laws were described in a straight forward informative manner and the content on law was simplified for the undergraduate level. There were not many analytical situations regarding the use or knowledge of laws. The test was simple and it lacked the use of analytical power. It was a direct test having only recall and recognition items, and, therefore, much discrimination among the students was not possible. This was deliberately done as there was no precedence for teaching of laws. Moreover, there is a general feeling that teaching of law is dry and boring. So to overcome these difficulties, investigator purposely made such video films and tests. No special method to teach and evaluate learning of laws was found by the investigator in her literature search. Hence, teaching and testing of knowledge both were rather simple. In future it could be tougher than this.

A more clear picture may be derived when a tight experiment is employed by exercising control on the variables and randomizing the sample. The methods of teaching and evaluating the learning can be more specific in a future study.

CHAPTER 5

SUMMARY AND RECOMMENDATIONS

Women's issues have assumed tremendous importance and have been attracting a lot of attention in recent years, specially in the context of social change and economic development. There is an awareness of the need for enhancing the status of women through education which is regarded as the most potent instrument for effecting a change in the unenviable and subjugated position occupied in our society by women.

Women in India suffer from a variety of social and economic disabilities which prevent them from exercising their human rights and freedom in society. During the last few decades, a number of legislations have been passed with a view to ensuring equality of status and opportunities for women. In practice, however, it seems it has eluded women. Therefore, it is important to educate the women about the radical changes in the law.

Reviews of the studies conducted established that awareness of women regarding laws is very poor. It was further revealed that a change was creeping slowly and steadily in policies of government, women's organisations and need to spread legal education is felt. A sizeable theoretical literature was available on effectiveness of T.V. and video but very limited literature was found on teaching college students through video.

There, is a need to develop systematic video film on "Women and Law". The amount of investigation, research on video film is limited which necessitated further exploration in this area. It is established that the law related course are strongly recommended for women. Although need to educate women about law is felt, a systematic beginning has not been done. Therefore, undertaking a study to develop the content of "Women and Law" to teach Home Science students assumes significance.

Thus, it is obvious that course "Women and Law" can play a catalytic role in bringing about social change which is also one of the ultimate aims of Home Science education.

Legal education in Home Science is considered more seriously than anything else because in recent years crime against women has assumed giant shape. Even facts related to figures on crime serve as an eye opener for Home Scientists whose activities are geared towards betterment of family, community and nation, keeping the women as their focus.

Undertaking a study to develop the content of course "Women and Law" in relation to the curriculum of Home Science assumes significance and should be given appropriate priority. Keeping the above justifications in mind, a study on "Developing a course and video instructional package on "Women and Law" and measuring the effectiveness of package with the students of Faculty of Home Science, Baroda", was undertaken.

MAJOR OBJECTIVES

1. To develop an effective introductory course on "Women and Law".
2. To develop video instructional package on "Women and Law".
3. To study the effectiveness of video package to teach "Women and Law" to the first year Home Science students in terms of performance of students on knowledge test.

NULL HYPOTHESES

1. There will be no significant difference in knowledge gain in terms of pre-post scores of the students according to the stream of study at higher secondary school.

2. There will be no significant difference in knowledge gain in terms of pre-post scores of the students according to the medium of instruction at school level.
3. There will be no significant difference in knowledge gain in terms of pre-post scores of the students according to the place of residence.
4. There will be no significant difference in knowledge gain in terms of pre-post scores of the students according to the inclination towards social science.
5. There will be no significant difference in knowledge gain in terms of pre-post scores of the students according to the family's legal exposure.
6. There will be no significant difference in knowledge gain in terms of pre-post scores of the students according to the social work background.
7. There will be no significant difference in knowledge gain in terms of pre-post scores of the students according to the mother's occupation.
8. There will be no significant difference in knowledge gain in terms of pre-post scores of the students according to the exposure to TV and Video.
9. There will be no significant difference in knowledge gain in terms of pre-post scores of the students according to the socio-economic status.
10. There will be no significant difference in knowledge gain in terms of pre-post scores of the students according to the overall modernity.
11. There will be no significant difference in knowledge gain in terms of pre-post scores of the students according to the personality.
12. There will be no significant difference in knowledge gain in terms of pre-post scores of the students according to level of academic achievement.
13. There will be no significant difference in knowledge gain in terms of pre-post scores of the students according to the English competence.

METHOD OF PROCEDURE

Developing Outline for the Course "Women and Law"

In order to develop the outline of the present course, content analysis of the course outline of the related courses was done. An outline was drawn in light of broad objectives of the course "Women and Law". The developed outline was validated by the experts and was revised according to their suggestions.

Planning for Experimental Teaching

The units for the experimental teaching were selected and five libraries were consulted for collecting subject matter for teaching. The subject matter obtained for the course "Women and Law" was then organised. Unit plans for teaching the experimental units were developed and were validated by the experts.

Preparation of Educational Video Films on

For preparation of the video films full length of scripts with a complete list of visual illustrations and accompanying sound was made.

Mode of Presentation

The mode of presentation of the content was as follows:

Topic of the Unit	*Title of the Film*	*Format*	*Type of the film*
Introduction	Introduction to Law	Documentary, Interview	Informative
Eve Teasing	Are you Eve teased?	Documentary, Interview	Informative
Inheritance	Law of Inheritance	Interview Illustrative talk	Informative
Dowry	Is Dowry legal?	Dramatization Illustrative talk	Persuasive Informative
Marriage	Marriage made easy with law	Dramatization Illustrative talk	Persuasive Informative
Divorce	Law of Divorce	Interview, Lecture	Informative
Rape	Trauma of Rape!	Lecture, Illustrative Talk	Informative

Mode of presentation of video films were decided mainly in such a way that it achieves the objectives and yet presentation is done in interesting and practical manner. Since the films were made to impart information about various laws related to women mainly informative approach was used in writing the scripts.

TOOLS FOR DATA COLLECTION

A battery of tools was prepared by the researcher to collect the required information. The data collection tool for each purpose was as follows.

Purpose	*Tool*
1. Background information	Questionnaire cum Checklist with structured items.
2. English language competence	Examination office records.
3. Academic Achievement	Office records.
4. Socio-economic status	Standardized Socio-Economic Scale prepared by Desai (1987).
5. Modernity	Scale to measure level of modernity adapted and standardized by Mehta et al (1974) from the original 'OM[1] Scale of Modernity for Indian conditions.
6. Personality	The personality inventory by A.Hafeez and V.S.Shantamani (1974).
7. Gain in Knowledge	Seven tests on "Women and Law" having recall and recognition items, True and False, Fill in the blanks. Multiple choice.

THE EXPERIMENTAL TEACHING AND DATA COLLECTION

The questionnaires were printed in different colours, one for each law. The experiment was conducted with 279 First Year Home Science students in the month of March and April 1993. For data collection, the groups formed by the Faculty office were used. The experiment was conducted by administering pre-test, experimental teaching and post-test on the students.

Personality, Modernity and Socio-economic scale were also administered. Data thus gathered, were scored using the predetermined keys for the respective research tools.

ANALYSIS OF DATA

The analysis of data was done in IBM-PC/AT 386 compatible computer system.

The various statistical procedure were used for the analysis of data. Keeping in view the objectives of the study the following statistical methods were used for analysing the data.

1. Frequency and percentage distribution.
2. Mean Scores.
3. Paired 't' test.
4. Analysis of covariance.

MAJOR FINDINGS

1. Majority of the students were from general stream having urban background with social science inclination and majority did not possess legal and social work background.
2. Majority of the respondents were modern and extroverts although their mothers were housewives.
3. Nearly equal percentages of respondents were having high as well as low exposure to TV and video.
4. Majority of students were from high socio-economic status and nearly 60 per cent had high English competence, but low academic achievement.
5. All the seven video films were effective as there was considerable increase in the mean scores of the students' achievement on post-test for all the seven video films.
6. Overall, the film "Trauma of Rape!" was found to be most effective and film on "Introduction to Law" was least effective.
7. The Science stream respondents gained significantly higher than the general stream respondents for all the seven video films.

8. There was significant difference in gain in knowledge of students from English medium school as they learnt more in comparison to the students from vernacular schools.
9. Respondents who had science inclination learnt significantly higher than the respondents having social science inclination.
10. The presence and absence of legal exposure had nothing to do with the knowledge gain. However, in some cases, the previous legal exposure of student's family raised this awareness.
11. The respondents from city learnt significantly higher from the film 'Are you eve-teased?' For rest of the films variable place of residence did not play any role.
12. The film 'Marriage made easy with law' was found most effective by the respondents whose mothers were housewives.
13. The effect of variable 'English competence[1] was found to be significant for all the seven video films.
14. The respondents from high socio-economic status gained significantly higher from the video films in comparison to students from middle and low socio economic groups.
15. There was no significant difference in learning, in relation to Social work background, TV and video exposure, Modernity, Academic achievement and Personality.

RECOMMENDATIONS

The investigator on the basis of her experience during experimentation and findings of the study recommends that :

1. A similar type of study can be conducted including control group and retention test.
2. A similar type of study can be conducted with other variables related to media utilization.
3. Production and validation of the video films on more laws related to women other than included in the present study can be tried out.

4. A comparative study of the effectiveness of the present video package in teaching formal and non-formal group of women can be conducted.
5. A similar type of study can be conducted with other samples like, students from different levels and specializations.
6. A similar type of study with contents other than "Women and Law" can be conducted.
7. A study can be taken up with other instructional strategies on the same topic.
8. The strategies having both software and hardware and components can be developed and tried out.

APPENDICES

APPENDIX-I

COURSE OUTLINE ON "WOMEN AND LAW"

DEPARTMENT OF EDUCATION AND EXTENSION FACULTY OF HOME SCIENCE M.S.UNIVERSITY OF BARODA

Credit 3

WOMEN AND LAW

Major Objectives

To create awareness and understanding among the students regarding laws concerning women.

Specific Objectives

1. To develop awareness and understanding among the students regarding personal laws related to women.
2. To develop awareness and understanding among the students regarding women and the criminal laws.
3. To develop comprehension among the students regarding women and the social welfare legislation.

Content

Unit-I

1. Introduction
1. Women and the Constitution
2. Directive Principles directly related to women.

2. *Personal Laws*

1. Hindu Marriage Act, 1955.
   Conditions of marriage
   Registration of marriage
2. Marital Relief and Divorce
   Judicial separation and divorce. Section 23 and 27
   Divorce and Mutual Consent.
3. Maintenance and custody of children
   Section 24 of the Hindu Marriage Act.
   Section 37 of the Special Marriage Act.
   Custody of Minor Children.
4. Inheritance and Succession
   Hindu Succession Act, 1956.

Unit-II

3. *Criminal Laws*

1. Procedural Laws
   Cognizable and Non Cognizable offence
   F.I.R.
   Bailable and non bailable offence
   Rights of an accused
2. Substantive Laws
   Eve teasing (Section 352 of IPC)
   Wife beating (Section 323 of IPC)
   Cruelty on married women (Section 498 A IPC)
   Rape (Section 375 of IPC)

Unit-III

4. *Woman and Social Welfare Legislation*

1. Dowry Prohibition Act/ 1961.
2. Medical Termination of Pregnancy Act, 1972.

SUGGESTED EVALUATIVE METHOD

The students will be able to recall and recognise knowledge and thus develop intellectual skills. Objective type test covering questions of True/False/Fill up the gaps, Multiple choice items, short answer type will be used to evaluate the students.

The students can be evaluated three or four times in a Semester.

SUGGESTED LEARNING EXPERIENCES

Teacher needs to plan the learning experience for the students so that the objectives can be achieved. The students will achieve educational objectives by interacting with the environment by role playing, quiz method, etc. Some examples of educational environment are–

1. Watching video film on laws related to women.
2. Video film followed by question-answer session by the students.
3. Writing summary of the video film on laws viewed by the class.
4. Talks from Resource person such as–
   (a) Person who has gone to the Court and have benefitted from the knowledge of law.
   (b) Lawyers and other law professionals talk and discussions on needs and problems of women and law.
5. Classroom discussion among teacher and students.
6. Reading text or reference books.
7. Writing assignment out of the class.
8. List reasons for including "Women and Law" in the Home Sciencecurriculum.
9. Writing essay on topics such as–
   (a) Importance of law for Indian women.
   (b) Constitution protects women.
   (c) Your rights in Criminal law.
   (d) Women's status: Myth and Truth.

SUGGESTED REFERENCES

1. Haksar, N. and Singh, A. (1986), Demystification of the law for women. 112,Lancer Press, New Delhi.
2. Sachidanand and Sinha, R.P. (1980), Women's Rights: Myth and Reality. Printwell Publishers, Jaipur.
3. Antony, M.J. (1989), Women's Rights. Clorion Books, Robo Printers, Delhi.
4. Desai, N. and Patel, V. Indian Women Change and Challenge in the International Decade 1975-1985. Popular Prakashan, Bombay.
5. Dhagamwar, V. (1980), Women and Divorce. Samaya Publication, New Delhi.

APPENDIX-II

CONTENT ON "WOMEN AND LAW"

WOMEN AND THE CONSTITUTION

Constitution is the fundamental legal document in a democratic society. It lays down the principles for the governance of a country. The Indian Constitution, which came in force on 26th Jan. 1950/ is no exception. It provides the framework for the governance of the country assigning roles to different institutions such as executive, legislature and judiciary. The social and economic aspects have been taken care of by the Preamble, which the State should endeavour to secure for its people. These ideals have been given concrete form by guaranteeing certain rights which the framers of the constitution considered fundamental.

Certain classes of persons, who, by themselves are not able to get the full benefit of the socio-economic change contemplated, have been given special protection.

While all provisions of the Constitution are applicable in equal measure to men and women, and can, therefore, be invoked by women for the assertion of their rights.

Part III and Part IV need special mention as they are the backbone on which protective legislation for women has been based. Part III of the Constitution recognises and confers fundamental rights to citizens. Of the various rights conferred in this part, there are two provisions which need to be mentioned as these are of special importance for women.

The first of these is the equality before law. Article 14 of the Constitution secures to every person equality before law and equal protection of law. Article 14 of the Constitution secure to every person equality before law and equal protection of law, this has been further elaborated that State shall not discriminate against any citizen on grounds of sex along with any other grounds.

However, the State has made special provisions for women under various laws like Factories Act, Mines Act, Plantation Labour Act, etc.

The other important provision, which is an extension of the principle of equality before law, is equality in the matter of employment or appointment under the State. Article 16(1) states that, "There shall be equality of opportunity for all citizens in matters of employment of appointment to any office under the State." Further, "No citizen shall, on grounds of religion, race, caste, sex, descent, place of birth, residence or any of them be ineligible or discriminated against in respect of any employment or office under the State. [(Article 16 (2)].

The importance of these provisions is that a woman has the same rights in the matter of employment under the State as a man. The State can not practice any discrimination on this count.

Apart from the rights guaranteed in Part III of the Constitution which have a special bearing on women, Part IV of the Constitution has some special provisions for the welfare of the women and for the improvement in their social and economic status.

In Article 38 and 51 which contain the Directive Principles, the Social and economic goals have been set with a view to fulfill the basic needs of the common man. In order to enable them to participate in the socio-economic development of the country, a climate has to be created for them to be equal partners in development with man, rather than being mere beneficiaries of developmental activities.

The sum and substance of the Constitutional provisions is that women stand on equal footing with men in all spheres of economic, social and political life of the country. Discrimination has been completely abolished on the ground of sex, and women belonging to different religions and races have the same status in the eyes of law.

MARRIAGES

Marriage is a sacrement in Hinduism and other major religions, except Islam where it is a mere civil contract.

India has several religions and each of them has separate rules and traditions to govern family law, called the Personal Law of that community.

Hindus are governed by Hindu Marriage Act, 1955. A Hindu in this context includes Buddhists, Jains, Sikhs and their denominations.

Muslims, Christians, Parsis and Jews have separate laws of their own.

With more and more love marriages between inter caste and inter religion, those youths who do not want to be ruled by any of these religious traditions, can conduct a 'Civil' marriage under the special marriage act, 1954.

Hindu Marriage

A great deal of importance was attached to marriage in ancient Hindu religion.

The Hindu law of marriage originated from ancient books traditions and Acts passed by Government in modern times.

The Act applies to all States except J & K (which has a separate law) and covers all Hindus.

A child whose only one parent is Hindu and the child is brought up as a Hindu, it will be a Hindu (which includes Buddhists, Jains and Sikhs).

Converts and reconverts are also Hindu.

The Act sets forth four essential conditions for a valid Hindu marriage. They are–

(1) Monogamy

(2) Sound mind

(3) Marriageable age

(4) Parties should not be too closely related.

A Hindu marriage may be solemnised in accordance with Shastric rites or the ceremonies of either party.

The law does not prescribe any specific rite because there are too many customs in this large country.

Saptapadi is the most comnon rite among the Hindus and this had been considered to be essential by ancient law givers. A marriage becomes complete when the couple take the seventh step.

Monogamy

Any man marrying again while his wife is living will be punished with fine and imprisonment upto seven years.

Sound Mind

An idioti lunatic man can not marry as he can not give valid consent.

Marriageable Age

The Bridegroom must be 21 years old and the bride 18 years.

Parties should not be Closely Related

The law prohibits marriage between close relatives unless the customs of both parties permit it.

Civil Marriage

In contrast to the religious marriage/the civil marriage requires no rites or customary ceremonies.

It costs only a few rupees. Civil marriages are governed by Special Marriage Act, 1954.

This Act is very progresed and therefore it is getting more popular.

Any boy and girl can marry each other if they satisfy the following conditions.

1. The boy must be of 21 years and girl of 18 years.
2. Bigamy is prohibited.
3. Each party should give consent to the marriage.
4. The boy and girl should not be close relatives. However, if the boy or the girl belongs to a community where customs permit marriage between them, this bar will not apply and they can conduct a civil marriage.

Procedure

If the couple want to get married under Civil Marriage Act, they should give notice to the marriage officer.

The marriage officer enters it in the Marriage Notice Book.

He publicises the intended marriage by affixing the notice prominently in his office.

This is an announcement as well as invitation for objections to the marriage, if any.

Any person may object to the marriage within 30 days of the notice alleging that the four conditions of a valid marriage described earlier are not fulfilled.

If there is no objection within 30 days, the marriage may be solemnised. He can overrule the objection if it is found baseless.

For a civil marriage, three witnesses are necessary, declaration couple and the three witnesses should sign a marriage before the marriage officer.

The marriage may be solemnised in the marriage office or in the neighbourhood.

It is compulsory under law for each to tell the other : "I take thee (name) to be my lawful wife/husband". This must be done in the presence of the three witnesses and the officer.

After the marriage, it is entered in the marriage Certificate Book in which the couple and the three witnesses will sign. This is complete proof that the marriage has taken place.

DIVORCE

There are some ground for seeking judicial separation and divorce common to Hindu marriage and civil marriage.

Unsound Mind

Either spouse can move the court for dissolving the marriage if the other spouse has been incurable of unsound mind or has been suffering continuously from mental disorder and the petitioner can not reasonably be expected to live with the other.

Leprosy

Leprosy as it is contagious and therefore the healthy spouse has good reason to seek divorce. The Indian Divorce Act and Parsi law do not recognise laprosy as ground for a separation or divorce.

Veneral Disease

Diseases which spread through sexual intercourse/is called veneral diseases. These V.D. diseases can be deadly also where as some may just cause discomfort.

According to doctors/V.D. can be contracted only through sexual contract. It cannot spread through toilet seats/water/ drinking taps, spoons/etc. though a victim may use these excuses.

Presumption of Death

Marriages under the Hindu Laws and Civil Marriages can be dissolved if one party is missing for more than seven years.

If the spouse "has not been heard of as being alive for a period of 7 years who would naturally have heard of it, had the party been alive, it is presumed that the spouse is dead".

The law does not explain the situation when the missing person returns and finds the other spouse married again.

Separation for more than a Year

If there was a decree for judicial separation, and neither party has resumed living together for one year or more, the marriage can be dissolved by either party.

This ground for divorce accepts the break-down of marriage as a good reason to dissolve it, though one spouse may like to prolong it.

Sometimes, such divorce can be "engineered" by one party. Suppose the husband commits a matrimonial offence like adultery, on that ground the wife gets judicial separation. After one year, the husband seeks divorce because there was no cohabitation.

The principle is that no Court can mend a hopelessly broken marriage.

WOMEN AND THE LAW OF INHERITANCE THE HINDU LAW OF SUCCESSION

Meaning of terms :

Before we go further it is perhaps wise to clarify a few terms :

1. A Will constitutes written directions given by a person of what is to be done to or with his property after his death; also called "Testament."
2. Testamentary-according to one's will.
3. Intestate-without leaving a will.

INHERITANCE BY WOMEN

Old Hindu Law

Before 1956, women's rights of inheritance were determined by the old traditional Hindu Law. Women were subjected to many disabilities under this law. Thus, a woman could have no rights in joint family property. Even property inherited from her husband was not totally within her disposal. The only property that was fully hers was what was known as "Stridhan".

Hindu Succession Act, 1956

This Act was a boldly reformative piece of legislation which has placed women at par with men where inheritance is concerned. Broadly, any person may make a will directing to whom his property is to go after his death, and may, if he so chooses/leave his property to a woman. It is when no will exists and when a person dies intestate that the law must lay down who are the people entitled to inherit. It is here that the Hindu Succession Act broke new ground.

Absolute Owners

A Hindu woman can now inherit property in the capacity of a widow, daughter, mother, etc. as full and sole owner without any limitations on her power to do as she pleases with her property.

Where a person dies without making a will his property devolves on his/her relatives "of the first degree", and failing them, on other relatives. Out of the twelve relations of the first degree/ eight are women, viz. widow, daughter, mother, widowed daughter-in-law and widowed grand-daughter-in-law, grand-daughter by a son who has died, and great-grand-daughter by a grandson who has died. If a son or daughter has died before the intestate, then the share of such son or daughter will devolve on their respective spouses and children.

RIGHTS OF FEMALE HEIRS

Widow

1. Under the Act, a widow inherits a share in her husband's property equally to that of a son.
2. A widow can even inherit her deceased husband's share in joint Hindu family property eventhough she is not considered a copartner.
3. She inherits the property absolutely, i.e. there are no limitations on her powers over it and she can pass it on to her own heirs.
4. A woman staying away from her husband, either because of judicial separation or because he has forsaken her, is a legal heir and entitled to inherit as a widow.
5. Unlike under the old Hindu law, immorality in a widow cannot operate so as to defeat her right to inherit.
6. Re-marriage by the widow, after inheriting does not divest her of the property inherited. In other words, she is not bound to return it.

Daughter

A daughter also inherits a share in her father's property equal to that of a son.

Mother

A man's mother is also in heir of the first degree and inherits a share equal to that of widow and/or children.

Right to Demand Partition

All female heirs of the first degree have a right to demand partition of the estate of the deceased.

SUCCESSION TO A WOMAN'S PROPERTY

Will

Every woman as the right to dispose of her property by will to whomsoever she pleases, without any restriction.

Intestate Succession

1. If a woman dies without making a will, her property will be inherited by her husband and children in equal shares.
2. If any child or children have pre-deceased her then the children of such child or children will inherit the share their parent would have got if he or she had survived the mother.
3. If a woman dies a widow and childless, the succession to her property is determined by the manner in which she acquired it:
    (a) If the property, (or part of it), was inherited from her parents, it is inherited by her own relations, i.e. mother, father, brother, sister, and their children.

    (b) If the property (or part of it) was inherited by her from her husband or his relatives (in-laws), her husband's relatives i.e. parents in law, brothers and sisters-in-law, are considered to be legal heirs.

    (c) If the property is self-acquired, it will be inherited by the heirs as follows.

    First, the heirs of her husband, if they fail then her parents, if they fail then her father's heirs, if they too fail, then her mother's heirs.

Your Rights in Criminal Law

Criminal law in our country is very elaborate and protects citizens in almost all circumstances. The Indian Penal Code lists crimes and specifies punishment for each of them.

F.I.R.

A criminal case starts with a citizen making a complaint to the Police. You can go to the Police and lodge First Information Report (F.I.R.). It need not be in writing. It is not necessary that you yourself should go to the Police, any one can lodge a complaint on behalf of another. When the complaint is made, the Police officer in charge will record it, read it over to you and give, a free copy of it after you sign the statement.

If the officer in charge refuses to record your complaint, you may write your complaint and send it to the Superintendent of Police.

Cognisable Offence

When the arrest can be made without warrant for an offence it is known as cognisable offence.

Non-Cognisable Offence

When the offence is one in which arrest can be made only by warrant of a magistrate. The officer will record the complaint and refer it to the local magistrate. The Police starts investigation only if the magistrate orders.

Procedure of Investigation

After the complaint the Police officer visits the spot for investigation and if necessary arrests the offender. After the investigation a report will be made to the magistrate who will decide whether to proceed with the case or dismiss the complaint. The witness is bound to answer all questions. The witness need not sign the statement they make.

The Police officer can not threat or make promise to obtain "confession".

The Cr.P.C. grants special protection to women, some of which are as follows:

Section 51(2) and 100 say that - If a woman is to be searched in connection with a crime, "the search shall be made by another woman with strict regard to decency".

Section 160 protects women from unnecessary harassment at the hands of policemen who make enquiries in criminal cases.

A woman should not go to the Police station to give evidence. The concerned policemen must meet her in her house.

Only a lady doctor or some one under her supervision can examine a woman involved in crime.

Harassment Through Courts

Sometimes cases are filed just to harass some one, some petitions with spicy details are given to the press. The victim has to take leave from work and attend the Court and pay lawyers fees. This type of harassment is called '*Vexatious litigation*'. It takes several forms.

Some one files a defamation case against you for saying something about him in an interview or a case of indecency is filed for a role you played on the stage or screen. The charges are often petty and false.

Moreover, the same case can be filed in several Courts in distance places to harass you. In such cases, you can point out the circumstances to a magistrate and ask him to stop the harassment. You can also move the High Court through a writ petition to prevent the abuse of the process of the courts.

Some States have laws to prevent vexatious litigation.

Misdeeds by Police

If the police harasses you unnecessarily, you can complain against them also. Searching, your house or person without apparent reason, taking away your property, taking bribes, etc. you may complain to the local magistrate against the erring policemen and get them punished with imprisonment.

Apart from complaining you can move to the High Court through a writ. You can also complain to the Police Commissioner or make it a public issue through the press.

Rights of an Accused

The law has given the citizens safeguards against harassment. Those who do not know these are likely to suffer at crucial times. It must be remembered that the law presumes that a person is innocent until he or she is proved guilty. The important rights of an accused are given below:

1. When a person has reason to believe that he may be arrested, he can ask for anticipatory bail. Under Section 438 of Cr.P.C. the court may grant such bail directing that in the event of arrest he/she may be released.
2. A person arrested must be immediately told the reason for the arrest.
3. Every accused has a right to consult a lawyer of his or her choice at all stages. (Section 303 Cr.P.C).
4. Any person arrested or detained shall be produced before a magistrate within 24 hours (Article 22 of the Constitution). This is to get his sanction to hold the accused for further time.
5. The accused has a right to get medically examined by a doctor to see whether he or she was injured or tortured by any one including the Police.
6. An accused cannot be asked cross-examined, the judge can ask for his explanation. An accused cannot be asked questions which incriminate him.
7. An accused has a right to fair and speedy trial and if he cannot afford a lawyer, the government must provide him a lawyer.
8. Hand cuffs can not be used unless the accused is a dangerous charcter. If hand cuffs are used, the Police must explain the reasons to magistrate.

Substantive Law

Every society has certain norms of behavior and any deviation from the accepted norms attracts censure from those who are authorized to enforece these norms. When the behavious is international and harms another person or property, it becomes an act punishable by law.

For our purpose we would confine ourselves to a discussion of only those offences, which are directed against woman or in which she is a victim. In the process, we would also touch upon various problems which a woman faces in her day to day existence in home and outside and the relief that is available to her, in case she desires to initiate action.

Eve Teasing

Eve teasing by itself is not an offence under any law at present. But a close reading of Section 294 and 354 of the Indian Penal Code would indicate that the substance of the act of eve teasing would be covered by them.

Section 294 states that "Whoever to the annoyance of others

(a) does any obscene act in any public place,

(b) sings, recites or utters any obscene song or words in or near any public place" is liable to be punished with imprisonment or with fine.

A girl or woman who feels annoyed by any obscene song or words can take recourse to the provisions of this Section and put up a complaint before, a police station. The offence is cognizable i.e. a police officer can arrest the offender without a warrant-but bailable.

A graver form of eve teasing is accompanies by the use of gesture indicating threat of use of force. Section 352 of the Indian Penal Code which provides the punishment in such a case.

Thus, it would be abundantly clear that simple eve teasing as well as eve teasing accompanied with gesture to use force are punishable under the existing provisions of the Indian Penal Code.

Wife Beating

Wife beating is not new but it is receiving more and more attention in recent years. It has, however, assumed new dimensions particularly because of the attention it has been receiving from the press and public.

Wife beating has not been included as an offence per se either in the Indian Penal Code or any other law. One, therefore, has to look for remedies under the general Criminal Law.

Beating in any form would be covered by the definition of "hurt" as given under Section 319 of IPC.

"Hurt"-Causing bodily pain, disease or infirmity to any person.

Person who intentionally hurts the other person can be punished with imprisonment for a period of one year or fine which may extent to Rs.1,000 or both under Section 323 of the IPC.

The offence is non-cognizable and bailable. It means that though the information about such an offence can be received by an officer-in-charge but he can not take any action unless he obtains an order of the Magistrate.

Beating may be simple i.e. slapping or it may cause severe hurt in the form of permanent impairment of limbs or leading to hospitallzation. Under Section 320 of IPC the following kind of hurts have been described as grievous.

1. Emasculation.
2. Permanent deprivation of the sight of either eye, ear.
3. Destruction, permanent disfiguration of the head, face, bone.
4. Any hurt which endangers life or which causes the sufferer to remain for twenty days in severe bodily pain or unable to follow his ordinary pursuit.

The punishment extends from seven years to ten years with fine depending upon the nature of instrument used for commission of offence.

The offence is cognisable but bailable.

Cruelty on Married Woman

Cruelty on married woman has been made a substantive offence by a newer Section 498-A in IPC by Criminal Law (Second Amendment) Act, 1983.

Cruelty means–

(a) Any willful conduct which would drive the woman to commit suicide or to cause grave injury or danger to life, limb or health of the woman.

(b) Harassment of the woman where such harassment is with a view to coercing her or any person related to her to meet any lawful demand for any property or valuable security or any person related to her to meet such demand.

The husband of the woman and his relatives can be punished.

A sentence of imprisonment upto three years can be awarded for the commission of this offence.

An important change in the rules of evidence has been introduced by the insertion of a new Section 113 A in the Indian Evidence Act by the Criminal Law Act, 1989.

According to ordinary rules of evidence, a fact has to be proved by the person who alleges. But there is a presumption about the existence of certain facts as an exception.

Section 113 A lays down an important rule in this matter. It says that–

(a) If a woman marriage, commits suicide within seven years of her

(b) her husband and relatives have subjected her to cruelty.

The presumption would be that such husband or the relative has abetted the suicide. The insertion of this section would help many married women plight as direct evidence in such a case is generally lacking.

OFFENCES RELATING TO MARRIAGE

More than 120 years ago, the British law makers had listed offences relating to marriage in the Indian Penal Code, the two most important ones being BIGAMY and ADULTERY. Though society has changed a lot, these provisions in Chapter XX of the Indian Penal Code (IPC) have not been updated. The result is that these provisions assume that wives are the property of their respective husbands and they have no personality of their own.

Bigamy

If a person conducts a second marriage, while the first marriage is still subsisting he or she would be guilty of bigamy under Section 494. The second marriage must also be conducted with ceremonies required by law or customs to make it bigamy. Just asserting that they were married would not be enough; both the first and second marriage should go through the essential ceremonies. The second marriage would be void, apart from being bigamy. The law of bigamy applies equally men and women.

A man who commits bigamy, very often pleads that the first marriage was not valid, so that he can get rid of his first wife, civil marriages, it is difficult for him to prove that the first marriage was invalid because it is registered. But religious marriages which are not always registered create problems of proof of the first marriage.

In many cases the first marriage cannot be proved legal and therefore, the first wife is thrown on the street. Scared of plight, many women do not go to the Court at all and live miserably with their bigamous husbands. Compulsory registration all marriages will solve this problem.

The punishment for bigamy is fine and jail upto seven years. If the person conceals the first marriage and induces another to another to marry him or heir it will be more severe form of bigamy. The concealment aggravates the crime. So the punishment will be jail up to ten years and fine.

In law, adultery is sexual intercourse with a married woman without her husband's consent or connivance. Therefore, sex with an unmarried woman, widow or even a married woman with her husband's consent is not adultery.

Section 497 says: "Whoever has sexual intercourse with a person who is and whom he knows or has reason to believe to be wife of another man without the consent or connivance of that man, such sexual intercourse (not amounting to the offence of rape) is guilty of adultery".

The husband's consent must be clear, though not necessarily in writing.

The husband's consent or connivance must be clear, though necessarily in writing. It is difficult to get direct evidence of adultery. Adultery is an offence against the husband of the woman, and not against woman herself. For instance, Mr. Singh has sex with Mrs. Agarmal without Mr. Agarmal's consent. In this case Mr. Agarmal can complain against Mr. Singh. That only a husband can prosecute his wife's lover.

Though Mrs. Singh can not prosecute anyone, she can seek divorce from her husband on the ground of adultery.

Punishment

The punishment for the crime is fine and jail upto five years. The man is not ordinarily arrested by the police.

The Criminal Procedure Code names those who can complain of offences relating to marriage. The general rule is that the Court will not take notice of an offence unless the complaint is made by some person aggrieved by the offence. But it is not always necessary that the offended woman herself should lodge the complaint.

If the husband commits bigamy, the following persons can lodge a complaint : the wife, her farther, mother, brother, sister or with the permission of the Court any other person related to her by blood, marriage or adoption, son or daughter or by her uncle or aunt.

Rape

Most women are not aware of the laws relating to rape and other sexual offences and the legal means available to them to punish the guilty.

Their ignorance is also exploited by police, lawyers and their opponents.

What constitutes the crime of rape?

Section 375 of the Indian Penal Code defines rape. According to this definition rape is committed when a man has sexual intercourse with a woman :

1. against her will,
2. without her consent, or,
3 with her consent, when her consent has been obtained by putting her or any person in whom she is interested in fear of death, or of hurt; or,
4. with her consent, when he by deception, make her believe that he is her unsoundness of mind or intoxi-nation, when she is incapable of understanding the consequences of her consent,
5. with or without her consent when she is under 16 years of age.

What constitutes sexual intercourse?

Some penetration, however slight, sufficient to constitute the sexual intercourse. The degree of penetration is immaterial.

Note: Consent should be taken before the intercourse and not after.

Sleeping woman, woman with unsound mind, intoxicated woman and girl below 16 is not considered to give valid consent.

When does sexual intercourse by a man with his own wife considered rape?

According to Section 375 of IPC sexual intercourse by a man with his wife below 15 years of age is considered rape. This will protect the children of immature age against sexual intercourse.

What must be proved by the prosecution in a case of rape?

The prosecution must prove that-

1. The accused had sexual intercourse with the woman.
2. The act of sexual intercourse was done without her consent or the consent obtained by threat, fraud, deception, intoxication, etc.

3. The accused was below the age of 16 years.
4. There was penetration.

What must you do, if you are victim of rape?

1. Immediately rush to the nearest doctor and get yourself examined.
2. File an F.I.R. in the nearest Police Station as early as possible. Ask for a copy of the statement recorded. (You have a legal right to get a copy of the F.I.R. recorded free of cost).
3. You can have a lawyer of your choice to consult your case.
4. Demand that the person who has raped be medically examined.
5. Do not change clothes or take a bath till the completion of the medical examination.
6. Keep the articles (clothes, slippers, spectacles, etc.) obtained from the accused in the custody of the police.
7. Go to the Police station accompanies by a male relative or friend.

NOTE

1. Delay in reporting the offence to the Police officer would cast doubt on the story of the victim.
2. Delay may lead to disappearance of medical evidence.
3. The F.I.R. can be lodged by anyone who has the knowledge of the offence.

Punishment for Rape

Normal punishment for rape is minimum 7 to 10 years imprisonment and maximum life imprisonment and fine.

Can the woman kill the rapist?

Section 100 (iii) of the IPC gives authority to a woman to kill her assailant, if he assaults her with the intention of committing rape.

Dowry

Dowry is a common phenomenon all over India. It may be given in cash or in kind or both. To curb this menace, the Dowry

Prohibition Act was passed in 1961. In the three decades of its existence there have been few convictions under the Act.

The Act has come up for widespread criticism in recent years.

What is Dowry under the Act?

According to Section 2 of the Dowry Prohibition Act, 1961, 'dowry' means any property or valuable security given or agreed to be given either directly or indirectly.

(a) by one party to a marriage to the other party to the marriage.

(b) by the parents of either party to a marriage or by any other person to other party to the marriage or to any other person.

It may be given before marriage or at the time of marriage or after marriage by the parties "as consideration for the marriage". The Act has been amended in 1984 and the word "consideration" has been replaced with "in connection with marriage".

Dover or mehr as applicable to the Muslims under their Personal Law has been excluded from the definition of dowry.

However, according to Section 3(2) which has been added by the amending Act, following cases are excluded from the purview of dowry–

(1) Presents which are given at the time of a marriage to the bride or bridegroom (without any demand having been made in that behalf). These presents should be entered in a list maintained in accordance with the rules made under the Act.

(2) Presents made by on behalf of the bride or any person related to the bride should be of customary nature. The value of such presents should not be excessive having regard to the financial status of the person by whom such presents are given.

Section 4 of the Act provides that the taking, giving or demanding of dowry have been made substantive offence under the Act, and have been made punishable with imprisonment and fine. Minimum imprisonment of 2 years and fine of Rs. 10,000/-.

Return of Dowry to Woman

Section 6 of the Act further provides that if the dowry is taken by any person other than the woman in connection with whose marriage it is given,. In case it was given at the time of marriage or afterwards it has to be returned to the woman within three months of the date of its receipt.

A new Section 3A has been inserted in the Act by an amendment made in 1984. The Court can order the recovery of an amount equal to the value of the property. The amount can be paid to the woman or her heirs. These provisions can help in the speedy recovery of the property due to a woman.

Cognizance of Dowry Offence by Police

The Dowry Act now provides that the Code of Criminal Procedure, 1973 would apply as if the offences were cognizable:

The investigation consists of the following steps–

1. Proceeding to the spot.
2. Ascertainment of the facts.
3. Collection of evidence relating to the offence.
4. Discovery and arrest of the offender/ with the order of the Magistrate.

The offence committed under the Act are to be treated as non-compoundable and bailable.

Cognizance of Dowry Offence by Court

The congnizance of the offence by the Court, according to Section 7 of the Act, can only be taken -

(a) on the basis of its own knowledge or a police report of the facts which constitute the offence.

(b) Upon a complaint by the person aggrieved by the offence or parent or other relative of such person or by a recognised welfare institution.

One welcome change is that any recognised welfare institution can complain on behalf of the victim. Earlier only a victim could complain.

When some States found that the law was being violated in hundreds of ways, they introduced amendments to make it more stringent in their respective areas. For instance, the States of Haryana, Punjab and Himachal Pradesh prohibit "display of gifts made at or before the marriage in form of cash, ornaments of articles". The Punjab law is more stringent : any person who serves to the marriage party more than two principal meals (lunch or dinner) shall be punished with six months in jail and/or fine upto Rs. 5,000/-.

To what extent these amendments will be able to give relieve to dowry victims and to eradicate the evil only time will be able to tell.

APPENDIX-III

BACKGROUND INFORMATION

Please give the following information. Fill in the details/encircle the number/number of your choice.

1. Name____
2. Roll No. ____
3. Stream in Higher Secondary:
    1. Arts
    2. Science
    3. Commerce
    4. Any other
4. Medium of instruction at school level:
    1. English
    2. Gujarati
    3. Any other
5. In which city/town/village you have been residing for last 3 years? If you are staying in a hostel, please mention the place where you stayed before coming to Baroda.

    Name of City____

    Town____

    Village____
6. Can you show your inclination for choosing special subject (Major) form the given five areas?
    1. F.N. (Food and Nutrition)
    2. C.T. (Clothing and Textiles)
    3. H.M. (Home Management)
    4. C.D. (Child Development)
    5. Ed. Ex. (Education and Extension)
7. Has someone in your family taken the following degrees?
    - LL.B. 1. Yes 2. No
    - LL.M. 1. Yes 2. No.

8. Has nay one from your family been involved in Social work?
   1. Yes 2. No
   If Yes, Who?
   1. Father
   2. Brother
   3. Mother
   4. Sister
   5. Any Other
9. Has any of your family member been involved in the following legal proceedings? Please tick mark the case filed for:
   1. The claim of dowry
   2. The inheritance of property.
   3. Rape
   4. Divorce
   5. Maintenance
   6. Eve teasing
   7. The claim of accident
   8. None
10. What type of occupation your mother has?
    1. Home making
    2. Employment (teaching , business, service)
11. Do you watch T.V. Programmes
    1. Yes 2. No.
12. Which type of programmes do you watch on T.V.?
    1. Film oriented (film, chitrahar, regional films etc)
    2. Entertainment (play, pop music, serials etc)
    3. Educational (U.G.C. telecast, quiz, educational documentaries, educational films etc)
13. Do you watch programmes of Star Track (through cable connection) on T.V.?
    1. Yes 2. No.
14. Which type programmes do you usually watch through cable connection?
    1. Star Plus
    2. Prime Sport

3. B.B.C.
4. Music T.V.
5. Zee T.V.
6. ATN
7. Films

15. Do you watch Video?

1. Yes 2. No

16. Where do you watch the video?

1. in your own house
2. by bringing it on rent
3. at friends place

17. Which type of programmes do you watch on video?

1. Film oriented
2. Entertainment
3. Educational

18. How much time do you spend in watching programmes? Please tick mark in the appropriate space.

Programmes	*Routine Days*			*Holidays/Sunday*		
	1-2hrs	*3-4hrs*	*5 or more hrs*	*1-2hrs*	*3-4hrs*	*5 or more hrs*
T.V.						
Cable						
Video						

APPENDIX-IV

A SOCIO-ECONOMIC STATUS SCALE

Name:______________________________Roll No.__________

Indices of SES and the marks assigned to different levels.

CASTE AND SUB-CASTE

Marks *Caste Groups*

1. Bhangi, chamar, and all other types of harijans all types of tribals.
2. Fishermen, thakerda, koli, waghri, rabari, pinjara.
3. Barber, potter, pathan, shoe-maker, gardener, washermen, mason, memon, malek, khoja, chhipa.
4. Carpenter, blacksmith, khatri, tailor, oil-merchant, Christian, shaikh, bariya.
5. Patidar, rajput, kshatriya, goldsmith, bohra, dowdibohra.
6. Brahmin, brahmakshatriya, C.K.P. kayastha, parsi, jew, jain, saiyed

VOCATION

Marks *Vocations*

1. *Unskilled workers:* daily wagers, labourers, gardeners, vegetable vendors, store-labourers, petrol pump workers, motor scooter cleaners, shoe menders, hand-cart pullers, leather-tanners, butchers.
2. *Semi-skilled workers:* cane-weavers, masons, radio, watch and scooter repairers, garrage-labourers, foremen, potters, barbers, oil-merchants, washermen, shoe makers, handicraftsmen, toy-makers, bus conductors, peons.
3. *Skilled workers:* Clerks, electricians, store-managers, telephone operators, typists, nurses, book-sellers, photographers, primary school teachers, or head-masters.
4. *Middle order vocations:* Insurance agents, university or college lecturers, high or higher secondary school teachers

or head-masters, pharmacists, contractors, Gujarati news correspondents, stenographers, government servants-class II.

5. *Professions:* Doctors, managers, engineers, lawyers, government servants-class I, university professors or readers, first class magistrates, IAS officers, architects, chartered accountants, principals of big colleges, newspaper editors, English newspaper correspondents, heads of big offices, heads of any type of big institutions.

EDUCATION

Marks	*Educational Qualifications*
0	Illiterate.
1	IV graders or those who are able to read and write.
2	Primary school graduates or seventh graders.
3	Secondary school graduates, technical school certificate holders (after IX grade), higher secondary school graduates those who have passed minimum VIII grade.
4	Any type of diploma of two years-holders, those who have completed three years college course of any faculty, homeopathy doctors, ayurvedic doctors, bone setters.
5.	Three to four year diploma holders, B.A., B.Com, B.Sc, L.C.P.S.
6.	B.Pharm., B.D.S., B.Ed., LL.B., M.A., M.Com., M.Sc, M.Ed., M.B.B.S., B.E., B.Tech., B.Sc. (Agri.)
7.	M.D., M.S., M.E., Ph.D., M.Pharm, C.A., F.R.C.S., M.D.S.

TOTAL MONTHLY INCOME

Marks	*Income range*
1	Less than Rs. 300
2	Rs. 300 to Rs. 500
3	Rs. 500 to Rs. 1,000
4	Rs. 1,000 to Rs. 2,000
5	Rs. 2,000 to Rs. 5,000
6	Rs. 5,000 to Rs. 10,000
7	Rs. 10,000 and above.

RESIDENCE

Marks	*Type of house, whether owned, rented or provided by employer*
0.	Living in the open
1.	A hut with a roof
2.	One or two rooms with shared bathroom
3.	Two rooms with independent bathroom and lavatory.
4.	An independent bungalow or flat or row house of three or four rooms
5.	An independent bungalow or a big flat having five rooms.
6.	A big bungalow having more than five rooms and a garden.

VEHICLE

Marks	*Type of vehicle used*
1.	Bicycle
2.	Scooter or motor cycle
3.	Rickshaw or tractor
4.	Motor car or station wagon

SCORING KEY OF THE SOCIO-ECONOMIC SCALE

The Scoring for SES Scale was done according to Desai's standardized scoring pattern (Appendix). As very few respondents were falling in "low" and "middle low" categories. These categories were merged to form, "low" category. The final categorization was done as follows:

Variables	*Category*	*Range of Score*
	High	26-35
SES	Middle	21-25
	Low	0-20

APPENDIX-V

SCORING KEY OF THE MODERNITY SCALE

To find out the level of overall modernity, the scoring was done according to the standardized scale. In all the questions 1-12, except 3, the first answer represents the modern and rest of all the answers are considered conservative and get score of '0'. For question number '3', the modern answer is second. For question number '13', a. higher number of problems is coded as the modern answer. The possible score was 0-13. It was categorized as :

Variable	*Category*	*Range of Score*
Overall Modernity	Modern	8-13
	Conservative	4-17

MODERNITY SCALE

Direction: Please tick mark (√) the most appropriate response according to your opinion.

1. Have you got highly concerned any time regarding social problems such as some communal riots?

   1. ( ) Frequently 2. ( ) Sometimes 3. ( ) Never

2. If schooling is freely available, how much schooling do you think children of people like yourself should have?

   1. ( ) Above 10 years 2. ( ) 8 to 10 years 3. ( ) 1 to 7 years

3. Two twelve years boys took time out from their work in the rice field. They were trying to figure out a way to grow some amount of rice with fewer hours of work.

   a. The father of one boy said,"The way to grow rice is the way we have always done it. Talk about change will waste the time but not help"

   b. The father of the other boy said "That is a good thing to think about. Tell me your thoughts about how we should change our ways of growing rice."

   Which father said the wise words?

   1. ( ) Statement "a" 2. ( ) Statement "b"

4. What quality should a man have to hold high office?
    1. ( ) High education and special knowledge.
    2. ( ) Coming from high family background.
    3. ( ) Devotion to the old and time honoured ways.
    4. ( ) Being the most popular among the people.
5. Which is most important for the future of this country?
    1. ( ) The hard work of people.
    2. ( ) Good planning on the part of the Government.
    3. ( ) God's help.
    4. ( ) Good luck.
6. Scientists in the universities are studying such things as what determines whether a baby is a boy or a girl and how is it that a seed turns into a plant. Do you think that this investigations are–
    1. ( ) All very good.
    2. ( ) All somewhat good.
    3. ( ) All somewhat harmful.
7. Which of these opinions do you agree more ?
    1. ( ) Some people say that it is necessary for a man and his wife to limit the number of children to be born so that they can take better care of those they have.
    2. ( ) Other say that it is wrong for a man and his wife to limit the number of children to be born.
8. Which of these kinds of news interest you most?
    1. ( ) World event.
    2. ( ) The nation.
    3. ( ) Your home town or village.
    4. ( ) Sports.
    5. ( ) Religious events or festivals.
9. If you were to meet a person who lives in another country a long way off, could you like his ways of thinking?
    1. ( ) Yes.
    2. ( ) No.

10. Do you think a man can be good without having any religion at all
    1. ( ) Yes
    2. ( ) No.
11. Do you belong to any organization? For example, social clubs, union, church, organizations, political party/ group or other groups.
    1. ( ) Yes
    2. ( ) No
12. How often do you get news and information from newspapers?
    1. ( ) Everyday 2. ( ) Few times a week
    3. ( ) Occasionally 4. ( ) Never
13. What are the biggest problems facing the country?

____

____

____

APPENDIX-VI

PERSONALITY SCALE

Extroversion-Introversion Inventory

Directions: Following are the items. Tick mark (√) under column 'Yes' if the item is applicable to you and if item is not applicable to you, tick mark (√) under column 'No'.

		Yes	*No*
1.	I enjoy social gathering or parties.	_____	_____
2.	My feelings change from happy to sad and sad to happy for no reason.	_____	_____
3.	I do not like to be leader at social functions.	_____	_____
4.	I can do good work even while people are looking on.	_____	_____
5.	I like to change from one type of work to another very often.	_____	_____
6.	I become conscious of being observed in the presence of superiors.	_____	_____
7.	I am not afraid of being punished.	_____	_____
8.	I like to have excitement (i.e. rousing or stimulation) in life.	_____	_____
9.	My memory is good.	_____	_____
10.	I am unhappy most of the time.	_____	_____
11.	I worry over possible misfortune.	_____	_____
12.	I blush (become red in face) very often in the presence of others.	_____	_____
13.	I do not have a wide circle of friends.	_____	_____
14.	One should act on suggestions quickly rather than stopping to think.	_____	_____

Contd...

	Yes	No
15. I do not like to keep quite when out in a group	_____	_____
16. Life is for getting pleasure.	_____	_____
17. I am not usually calm and collected most of the time.	_____	_____
18. I do not easily get tired of meeting people and talking to them.	_____	_____
19. I would prefer to stay at home rather than attend a social function or party.	_____	_____
20. I do not like public speaking.	_____	_____

SCORING KEY OF THE EXTROVERSION-INTROVERSION INVENTORY

Items		*Yes*	*No*
1.	I enjoy social gathering or parties.	_____	_____
2.	My feelings change from happy to sad and sad to happy for no reason.	_____	_____
3.	I do not like to be leader at social functions.	_____	_____
4.	I can do good work even while people are looking on.	_____	_____
5.	I like to change from one type of work to another very often.	_____	_____
6.	I become conscious of being observed in the presence of superiors.	_____	_____
7.	I am not afraid of being punished.	_____	_____
8.	I like to have excitement (i.e. rousing or stimulation) in life.	_____	_____
9.	My memory is good.		
10.	I am unhappy most of the time.	_____	_____
11.	I worry over possible misfortune.	_____	_____

Contd...

Items	Yes	No
12. I blush (become red in face) very often in the presence of others.	____	____
13. I do not have a wide circle of friends.	____	____
14. One should act on suggestions quickly rather than stopping to think.	____	____
15. I do not like to keep quite when out in a group.	____	____
16. Life is for getting pleasure.	____	____
17. I am not usually calm and collected most of the time.	____	____
18. I do not easily get tired of meeting people and talking to them.	____	____
19. I would prefer to stay at home rather than attend a social function or party.	____	____
20. I do not like public speaking.	____	____

EXTROVERSION-INTROVERTING INVENTORY

Author	: V.S. Shanthamani and A. Hafeez
Availability	: Authors, Department of Industrial Management Indian Institute of Science, Bangalore-12.
Time Required	: No time limit. It takes about 10 minutes.
Level	: English knowing adults.
Main Features	: This inventory has 20 items of which 10 items each relate to Extroversion and Introversion.
Scoring	: The total number of items answered in the direction of the trait for each scale separately is the score.
Reliability	: Split-half reliability was found to be .35 for extroversion, significant at .01 level and .29 for introversion significant at .05 level.
Validity	: Construct validity for extroversion was found to be .72 and for introversion it was .68.
Norms	: Percentile norms have been developed on 200 employed engineers.

Bibliography

Agarwal, B.C. Need Assessment Study in Kheda District. Unpublished Technical Report, Space Application Centre-ISRO, Ahmedabad, IS74.

———(1976), Research and the TV System. *Reprint from Vidura,* Vol. 13, No.6, December.

———(1985), UNESCO/BRU Project Report on Video flow in India. Development and Education Communication Unit-ISRO. Space Application Centre, Ahmedabad.

Agarwal, B.C. and Chandiram, J. (1982), Towards Equality: Women in Indian TV. Unpublished paper, Media Asia, p. 162-163.

Anderson, H.R. (1976), Selecting and Developing Media for Instruction. Van Nostrand Reinhold Co. Inc.

Antony, M. J. (1989), Women's Rights. Clorion Books. Robo Printers, Delhi.

Arora, H. (1975-76). ACcomparative Study of the Problems of English Background and the Facilities Enjoyed by the High and Low Achievers of 1st, 2nd and 3rd Year of the Faculty of Home Science.

Dissertation (M.Sc.)-M.S. University, Baroda, 1977. BAKER, E.L. and POPHAM, W.J. Value of pictorial embellishments in a tape slide instructional program. A.V. Communication Review, Southern University Press, Missoula Montana, 1965 N. 13.

Barbro, O.H. (1989),Violence Against Women. Women and Health. 13 (3-4), 1988, pp. 151-158. Studies on Women Abstracts, Vol. 7, No. 3.

Barve, M.V., Preparation and Testing of Filmstrips for the Teaching of Science-A Course in Standard IX and a Study of their Comparative

Effectiveness in Teaching Learning Process as Compared to Traditional Practice.

Ph.D. Edu., SNDT Univ. (1986), cited in Buch, M.B. (Ed) Fourth Survey of Res, in Edu.; CASE, Baroda, 1991.

Best, J.W. (1983), Research in Education. Prentice Hall of India Pvt. Ltd., New Delhi.

Bhagat, R. (1988), Impact of Mass Media on Farm Women, A Study. *Kurukshetra*. August.

Bhoite, A. (1988), Sex Ratio and the Status of Women in India. *Ahfad Journal*, 5(7).

Bloom, B. Ed. (1965), Taxonomy of Educational Objectives. Handbook 1, Cognitive domain. David McKay Co., New York.

Bloom, B.S. *et al.* (1971), Mastery learning. In: SHULMAN, L. ed. Review of Research in Education. Peacock Publishers, Itasca, Illinois.

Blueprint of Action Projects and National Plan of Action for Women. National Document. NIPCCD. Delhi, 1976.

Bruner, J.S. (1962), The Process of Education, in TABA H. Curriculum Development, Theory and Practice. Harcourt Brace and World/ New York.

Buch, M.B. ed. (1991), Fourth Survey of Research in Education, Baroda. Centre for Advance Study in Education, Faculty of Education and Psychology, M.S. University.

Chandra, A. (1978), Introduction to Home Science. Metropolitan Book Company Pvt. Ltd., New Delhi.

Chandra, A. and Chaudhari, D. (1978), Report of the Survey of Objectives of Home Science Colleges in India. In: A. Chandra. Introduction to Home Science. Metropolitan Book Co. Pvt. Ltd., New Delhi.

Chandra, A. and Saxena, T.P. (1979), Style Manual for Writing Thesis, Dissertations and Papers in Social Sciences. Metropolitan Book Co. Pvt. Ltd., New Delhi.

Chandra, A., Shah. A., and Joshi, U. (1989), Fundamentals of Teaching Home Science. Sterling Publishers Pvt. Ltd., New Delhi.

Chandra, A., Shah, A. and Thomas, A. (1987), An Experiment in Imparting Family Centred Knowledge to the Rural and Urban Adolescent Girls and Women Through Video Tapes. Project

Report, Department of Education and Extension, Faculty of Home Science, M.S.University, Baroda.

Chatterji, S.A. (1988), The Indian Women's Search for an Identity. Vikas Publishing House, Delhi.

Cherian, A. (1986), A Content Analysis of the Selected Health and Hygiene, Nutrition and Family Planning Programmes of Pij Television and Its Impact on Acquisition of Knowledge by Rural People of the Selected Villages of Kheda District. Thesis (Ph.D.), Department of Education and Extension, Faculty of Home Science,M.S. University, Baroda.

Chetanlal, N. Relative Effectiveness of Graphic Aids and Projected Aids Enriched with Museum Experiences, in Teaching Food and Digestion to VIIIth Standard Students of Navrachana Higher Secondary School, Baroda.

Dissertation (M.Sc), Department of Education and Extension, Faculty of Home Science, M.S. University, Baroda. 1987.

Chopra, N. (1989), Audience Profile-II. Facilities Available in the Faculties of the M.S. University of Baroda.

Educational Media Research Centre, Gujarat University, Ahmedabad, 1989.

Dagg, I.A. and Thompson, J.P. (1988), Miseducation: Women and Canadian Universities. Ontario, OISE Press, ISBN (Paper back).

Dale, E. (1969), Audiovisual Methods in Teaching. 3rd edition. The Dryden Press, Holt, Rinchart and Winston, INC..

Decade for Women-World Conference. Nairobi, Kenya. July 1-985. Report by Centre for Women's Development Studies. 1986, New Delhi.

Desai, K.G. (1987), The Preparation and Standardization of a Socio-economic Status Scale in Gujarati. *J. of Educational and Psychology,* 44(4). Jan.

Desai, N. and Patel, V. (1985), Indian Women Change and Challenge in the International Decade 1975-1985. Popular Prakashan, Bombay.

Devdas, R.P. (1959), Textbook of Home Science. Indian Council of Agricultural Research, New Delhi.

Devdas, R.P. (1958), The Meaning of Home Science. Coimbatore, Sri Avinashilingam College.

Dhagamwar, V. (1987), Women and Divorce. Somaya Publication, New Delhi.

Dosi, J.K. (1983), Television for Development. *Journal of the Council for Social Development,* 13 (4).

Dowry Death Case Set a Record. (*Hindustan Times,* Delhi, 25 Nov. 1987). in *Legal News and Views.* Vol. (12), 1987.

Dowry Deaths. *Hindustan Times* (Delhi). 12 Aug. 1989.

Dua, M.S. (1980), Themes in Indian Communication. Metropolitan Book Co. (P) Ltd., New Delhi.

Eva, I. (1979), Role of the University in the Women's Movement. Seoul, Korea. 1978. Proceedings. Ed. by Eva I. Shipstone and Noroh Shipstone. Lucknow, The Asian Women's Institute.

Fougeyrollas, P. Television and the Social Education of Women. Reports and Papers on Mass Communication. UNESCO. No.50. (Year not mentioned).

Garrett, H.E. (1979), Statistics in Psychology and Education. Vakils, Feffer and Simons Ltd., Bombay.

Gore, M.S. (1988), Education for Women's Equality. Centre of Women's Development Studies, New Delhi.

Goswami, A. (1986), Video Utilization by Selected Homemakers of Baroda City and their Opinion Regarding its Impact on Family Life. Dissertation (M.Sc), Department of Education and Extension, Faculty of Home Science, M.S. University, Baroda.

Gupta, A. (1990), Production and Validation of a Video Film on Selected Voluntary Organizations Working for Women in Baroda City. Dissertation (M.Sc), Department of Education and Extension, Faculty of Home Science, M.S. University, Baroda.

Gupta, A. (1991), To Produce a Video Film on "Puppetry" to Instruct the Home Science College Students and Testing its Effectiveness in Terms of Gain in Knowledge. Dissertation (M.Phil.) Department of Education and Extension, Faculty of Home Science, M.S. University, Baroda.

Gupta, V. (1990), A Comparative Study of the Effectiveness of Video Films Regarding Conservation and Purification of Water in Urban and Rural Schools, Vadodara. Dissertation (M.Sc), Dept. of Home Science Education & Extension, Faculty of Home Science, M.S. University, Baroda.

Haksar, N. and Singh, A. (1986), Demystification of Law for Women. Lancer Press, New Delhi.

Handbook of Policy and Related Documents on Women in India. Published by National Institute of Public Co-operation and Child Development. Delhi, 1988.

Hanrahan, J.J. (1981), An Analysis of the Life Style Characteristics of Viewers of Selected Television Program Types. Abstract: International Piss, of Humanities and Soc. Sci. 42 (1). July.

Harbison, F. (1977), Relationship Between Communication Technology and Development. In TEHERANIAN, M. HAKIMA, F. VIDALE, M. ed. Communication Policy for National Development Routledge and Kegan Paul, London, Henley and Boston.

Hazarika, D. (1991), Employed Women's Traditional and Modern Homemaking Responsibilities in Association with their Physical Facilities, Attitude and Problems and Inferences for Home Science Curriculum.

Thesis (Ph.D.), Department of Education and Extension, Faculty of Home Science, M.S. University, Baroda, 1991.

Hendrix, C.J. (1980), An Evaluation of the Contribution of Video Tape Self-Viewing, Role Playing and Counsellor Feedback in Learning Job Interview Skill. Dissertation Abstract International. 41 (5), Nov.

Hilary, A. (1987), Justice Unbalanced: Gender, Psychiatry and Judicial Decisions. Milton Keynes, Open University Press, ISBN.

Hilda, Taba. Curriculum Development-Theory and Practice. Harcourt, Brace and World, INC., New York, 1962, p. 293.

Hills, P.J. (1982), A Dictionary of Education, Leicester, Routledge and Kegan Paul, .

Hopkinson, P. (1971), The Role of Film in Development. Report and Paper on Mass Communication. (64). UNESCO, pp. 11-14, 28-30.

India, National Perspective Plan for Women 1988-2000 AD. Report of the Core Group: Department of Women and Child Development. New Delhi, Ministry of Human Resource Development, 1988.

India, Mass Media in India. Research and Reference Division, Ministry of Information and Broadcasting, Government of India, 1979-80.

India, Ministry of Human Resources Development. National Policy on Education. New Delhi, May, 1986.

India, University Grants Commission, Report for the year 1985-1986. Presented to the Government of India in Compliance with Section 18 of the UGC Act. New Delhi, 1956.

India, University Grants Commission, Guidelines for Under-graduate programmes in Home Science, New Delhi, Aug. 1984.

Inkles, Alex. Scale on Adaptation to Modernity. In: Udai Pareek, ed. Handbook of Psychological and Social Instruments, Baroda, Samasthi, 1974.

Inkeles, A. and Smith, D.H. (1974), Becoming Modern, Individual Change in Six Developing Countries, 0-M12. The Short Form. Huneumann Educational Books Ltd. London.

Jahan, R. (1983), Family Violence and Bangladesi Women: Some Observations. Women for Women. Collected Articles. Latifa Akand and Roushan Jahan. Dhaka.

Joshi, U. (1988), Effectiveness of Teaching a Course 'Introduction to Home Science Education and Extension' Through Multimedia Strategies to the First Year Home Science Students of the Faculty of Home Science, Baroda, in Relation to the Selected Students Characteristics. Thesis (Ph.D.), Department of Education and Extension, Faculty of Home Science, M.S. University, Baroda.

Joshi, V., Menon, G. (1986), Research on Women's Education in India: A Review. Perspectives in Education, 1986, Vol. 2, No. 2, 77-98. KAUSHAL, A. The Impact of Television Viewing in Terms of Gain in Knowledge, Change in Opinions and Change in the Amount of Time Spent in Household and Outside Activities.

Dissertation (M.Sc), Department of Education and Extension, Faculty of Home Science, M.S. University, Baroda, 1986.

Kerr, J.F. (1968), Changing Curriculum. University of London Press, London.

Kumar, K.J. (1981), Mass Communication in India. Jaico Publishing House, Bombay.

Kundu, R. (1980), A Study of Selected Characteristics of the Students of the Faculty of Home Science, Baroda, in Relation to their Academic Achievement. Dissertation (M.Sc.). Department of Education and Extension, Faculty of Home Science, M.S. University, Baroda.

K. Vasanthi Devi (1985), Women's Education for Social Change. In the University News. Oct 8.

Lampkin, E.C. (1976), Adolescent Television Use as a Possible Socialization Agent. A Cross Cultural Comparison. Abstract; International Dissertation of Humanities and Soc. Sci., 37(2). Aug.

Laul, V. (1989), A Comparison of Video Cassettes Alone and Along with Hand out Regarding Adequate Nutrition at Low Cost, in Lal Bahadur Shashtri School, Harni Road, Vadodara.

Dissertation (M.Sc.)—Dept. of Home Science Education & Extension, Faculty of Home Science, M.S.University, Baroda, 1989.

Mandal, S. (1991), Identification of the Academic and Non-academic Problems Related to English Faced by the Students of the Faculty of Home Science, Baroda in Relation to the Selected Variables. Dissertation (M.Sc), Department of Education and Extension, Faculty of Home Science, M.S. University, Baroda.

Mandal, S. (1992), A Comparative Study of the Effectiveness of Three Instructional Strategies in Teaching Selected Aspects of the M.S. University, Baroda. Dissertation (M.Phil.), Dept. of Home Science Education & Extension, Faculty of Home Science, M.S.University, Baroda.

Mehta, A.S. (1992), The Laws of Crimes-Research Paper Presented in the Symposium on "Sex-bias in Indian Laws" by Indian Science Congress Association. Jan.

Mehta, M. (1988), The Use of television for Higher Education under the Countrywide Classroom Project of UGC in India. A Mimeographed Report. Educational Media Research Centre, Gujarat University, Ahmedabad.

Mehta, V., Desai, N. and Sharma, K. (1989), Audience Response Programme on Digital Electronics-III. Educational Media Research Centre, Gujarat University, Ahmedabad.

Mehta, P., Sinha, B.P., Gokulnathan, P.P. (1974), 'Scale for Level of Modernity', ed. Pareek, U., Rao, V.T. Handbook of Psychological and Social Instruments. Samasthi.

Majority of Women Unaware of Rights. (*Hindustan Times*, Patna, 7 Dec. 1987) in *Legal News and Views*. 1987, Vol. XII (12).

Mehta, V. and SHARMA, K. (1989), Pretesting Report-Invisible Work-II, 1989. Educational Media Research Centre, Gujarat University. Ahmedabad.

Menon, M.B. (1984), Evolving a Multi Media Approach to Teaching at Post Graduate Level. Thesis (Ph.D.), CASE, M.S. University, Baroda.

Miller, M.L. (1982), A Pragmatic Model for Curriculum Development. In Dissertation Abstracts International, Vol. 42, No. 10, April.

Mittal, L.N. (1992), Women's Studies in Curriculum Development. University News, April 20.

Mohanty, J. and Rath, A. (1990), Countrywide Classroom Television Programmes-An Appraisal Study, 1988. *University News*, Vol. XXVIII (50). Dec. 10.

Mohanty, J. and Sahu, H. (1991), Countrywide Classroom Television Programme-An Appraisal. *University News*, Vol. XXVIII (52). August 5.

More Dowry Victims Seeking Redressal. (Patriot, Bombay. 12 Jan. 1988) in *Legal News and Views*, Vol. II (2), 1988.

Myrdal, G. (1969) Iri: PILLAI, J.K. Empowering Women in India. *University News*, 28 (47), Nov. 1990: 1-5.

National Seminar on Legal Aid for Women-The Role of Voluntary Organizations, New Delhi, 1986. Proceedings. University of Delhi, Jan. 1986.

National Education Policy-1986 and Programme of Action, Aifucto Publication, Delhi, 1990.

Pillai, J.K. (1990), Empowering Women in India. *University News*. 28 (47), Nov., 1-5.

Programme of Action (N.P.E. 1986) Published by Ministry of Human Resource Development, Department of Education, New Delhi, 1986.

Rai, U. (1989), A Matter of Honour. *Times of India* (Bombay). 19 Nov.

Rape Used as 'Class Weapon[1] Report of Central Executive Committee. *Hindustan Times*, (New Delhi). June 28, 1988.

Report: Seminar on Women's Development and Legal Literacy. Department of Home Science, Amravati University. 18th -19th Jan. 1990.

Report on the Education Commission, Government of India, Ministry of Education, 1964-66.

Richardson, L. and Callahan, G. (1951), How to Write for Homemakers. The IOWA State College Press. Ames IOWA.

Roe, Anne. The Psychology of Careers. New York : Harper and Sons, Inc. 1967.

Sachidanand and Sinnha, R.P. (1984), Women's Rights: Myth and Reality. Printwell Publishers, Jaipur.

Second National Conference on Women's Studies. Indian Association for Women's Studies. Trivendrum, April 9-12, 1984. Mimeographed.

Sen, M. (1988), "Biased Laws Bar Women's Progress". *Times of India*, India, (New Delhi), Jan. 1.

Seth, I. (1983), A Study of Effectiveness of Educational Television, the Educational Development of Primary School Children.

Thesis (Ph.D.)-M.S. University, Baroda, 1983.

Seymour (1973), "Video Cassettes : A Technology Whose Time has Come" Cited in Educational Technology, Vol. XIII, No. 4, Pg.14, A Magazine Pub. 140 Sylran Avenue, Englewood Clifds, New Jersey. April.

Shah, A. and OJha, S. (1990), Women and Law. (A Compilation of Speeches). The Home Science Education and Extension Alumni Association. Dept. of Home Science Education & Extension, M. S. University of Baroda.

Shanthamani, V.S. and Hafeez, A. (1974), Department of Industrial Management Indian Institute of Science, Bangalore.

SHASTRI, B. (1990), Views on Visual Profile. Research Report Educational Media Research Centre, Gujarat University, Ahmedabad. April.

Shehla, Z., Jhani, J. and Asma, J. (1982), Muslim Laws and their Implementation in Pakistan. Islamabad, Women's Division Cabinet.

Sharma, K., Hussain, S., and Sahaya, A. (1985), Women in Focus a Community in Search of Equal Roles. Orient Longman Ltd., Hyderabad.

Sharmskati: Report of the National Commission on Self-Employed Women and Women in the Informal Sector, 1988.

Singh, A.K. and Dutt, S.S. Women and Development-Promise and Realities. New Delhi, Centre for Women's Development Studies. (Year not mentioned).

Sondhi, K. (1981), Problems of Communication in Developing Countries, Vision Books Pvt. Ltd., New Delhi.

Soon, T.E. (1989), Home Science Economics-A Catalyst for Change. Speech Delivered at the Asian Regional Association for Home Economics Biennial Conference. Singapore, July, pp. 1-13.

Srivastava, S. (1988), Legal Regulation on Women's Status in the Family, 1988. Mimeoqraphed. Paper read at the National Workshop on Enforcement Machinery and Women. Delhi/ NIPCCD, Feb.

Stanton, G. P. (1974), An Effect Analysis of Media and Message Interaction on Information Gain in Learning Environment. Ph.D. Denven U. Diss. Ab. Int.

Stokland, T., Vajrathon, M. Nicol, D. Creative Women in Changing Societies: A Quest for Alternative. Transnational Publishers, Inc. Dobbs Ferry, New York.

Taba, H. (1962), Curriculum Development: Theory and Practice Harcourt, Brace and World, Inc. New York.

Times of India Research Bureau. Statutory Panel for Women. *Times of India* (Ahmedabad) 5th May, 1990.

Towards Equality: Report of the Committee on the Status of Women in India. NIPCCD, Delhi. 1974.

Thomas, A. (1982-83), Effect of Organization of Content on Learning a Course Mass Communication in Home Science by First Year Home Science Students, Faculty of Home Science, M.S. University of Baroda.

Thesis (Ph.D.), Department of Education and Extension, Faculty of Home Science, M.S. University, Baroda, 1984.

Tiwari, N. Information Needs of the TV Viewing Urban Homemakers of Baroda City and their Opinions Regarding the Improvement in the Quality of TV Programmes.

Dissertation (M.Sc), Dept. of Home Science Education & Extension, Faculty of Home Science, M.S. University, Baroda, 1985.

Utilising Law and Legal Process for Women's Development, New Delhi, 1987. Proceedings. Legal Literacy Project. Dept. of Adult, Continuing Education and Extension. University of Delhi, Jan. 1987.

Verma, K.K. (1974), Need Assessment Study in Karnataka and Andhra Pradesh. Unpublished Report, Space Application Centre-ISRO, Ahmedabad.

Vikasini, Atrocities Against Women is a Worldwide Phenomenon: Some Facts. (Data Compiled from Tribune and Local Newspapers).

Centre for Women's Development, New Delhi, Vol. 2, No. 5, July/ Sept. 1989.

Warwick, D. (1975), Curriculum Structure and Design. University of London Press, London.

Women and Violence-Various Manifestation. Report of the National Seminar. Patna, Women's Development Studies, 1989.

Women Demand Equal Rights. Reported in The *Times of India,* Ahmedabad, March 9, 1990.

"Women, Religion and Family Law", Asian Women's Conference Report, Bombay, Dec. 16-20, 1987.

Woods, V.M. The Value of Home Economics Curricula in Higher Education as Perceived by Graduates.

Thesis (Ph.D.)—Purdue University, 1983. Disser. Abstr. International, 44 (9), March 1984.

Yashpal (1983), From Here to Where? In Joshi, S.R. ed. Feature Film on TV, ed. Space Applicatioin Centre-ISRO, Ahmedabad.

Index

SCORING KEY OF THE EXTROVERSION-INTROVERSION INVENTORY

	Items	*Yes*	*No*
1.	I enjoy social gathering or parties.	✓	
2.	My feelings change from happy to sad and sad to happy for no reason.	★✓	
3.	I do not like to be leader at social functions.		✓
4.	I can do good work even while people are looking on.		✓★
5.	I like to change from one type of work to another very often.	✓	
6.	I become conscious of being observed in the presence of superiors.		✓★
7.	I am not afraid of being punished.	★✓	
8.	I like to have excitement (i.e. rousing or stimulation) in life.	✓	
9.	My memory is good.		✓★
10.	I am unhappy most of the time.		✓
11.	I worry over possible misfortune.	★✓	
12.	I blush (become red in face) very often in the presence of others.	★✓	
13.	I do not have a wide circle of friends.		✓
14.	One should act on suggestions quickly rather than stopping to think.		✓★
15.	I do not like to keep quite when out in a group.	✓	
16.	Life is for getting pleasure.		✓★
17.	I am not usually calm and collected most of the time.	✓	
18.	I do not easily get tired of meeting people and talking to them.	★✓	
19.	I would prefer to stay at home rather than attend a social function or party.	✓	
20.	I do not like public speaking.	✓	

✓ Extrovert ★✓ Introvert

EXTROVERSION-INTROVERTING INVENTORY

Author	:	V. S. Shanthamani and A. Hafeez
Availability	:	Authors, Department of Industrial Management Indian Institute of Science, Bangalore-12.
Time Required	:	No time limit. It takes about 10 minutes.
Level	:	English knowing adults.
Main Features	:	This inventory has 20 items of which 10 items each relate to Extroversion and Introversion.
Scoring	:	The total number of items answered in the direction of the trait for each scale separately is the score.
Reliability	:	Split-half reliability was found to be .35 for extroversion, significant at .01 level and .29 for introversion significant at .05 level.
Validity	:	Construct validity for extroversion was found to be .72 and for introversion it was .68.
Norms	:	Percentile norms have been developed on 200 employed engineers.